Ivy
Book

The Ivy Book

The Growing and Care of Ivy

SUZANNE WARNER PIEROT

- *Second Edition*
- *Revised and updated plant identification*
- *Schedule for an Ivy Show*

Garden by the Stream
33 Hickory Road
Willow, New York 12495

Library of Congress Catalog Card Number: 95-78345
First printing 1995
ISBN Number 1-887738-00-2
Printed in the United States

Dedicated with gratitude
to
members of

The American Ivy Society

Contents

Photographs

Sabina Mueller Sulgrove
The American Ivy Society
David Whitley
Michael Mullally
Robert Reef - Prints

Cover Art   Aleta Pahl

 *Preface*

IT HAS been 21 years since "The Ivy Book, the Growing and Care of Ivy and Ivy Topiary" was published. So much has happened in the world of ivy, and there are so many new ivy collectors that I was asked to bring out a second edition which would include some of the ivies that weren't available before.

Eliminated from this edition is the section devoted to making a topiary. In 1974 I helped pioneer the idea of portable topiary made from ivy and very little information was available. Since that time, several fine books have been published, notably Longwood Garden's "The New Topiary", by Patricia Riley Hammer and "The Complete Book of Topiary", by Barbara Gallup and Deborah Reich.

In its place I now include a chapter on Staging an Ivy Show. With the permission of the Eastern Chapter of The American Ivy Society I am reprinting in its entirety the show schedule for their 1994 Ivy Show. You will get from it most of the information you need for staging your own show.

Deciding which ivies to include in the chapters on identification was not easy. There are now well over 400 cultivars known by the experts, but many of these are very hard to find. Therefore, in my selection process I chose only those that are readily available, perhaps not at your local nursery, but certainly from ivy specialists. A list of these sources is included at the end of the book.

In 1974 I devised a method of classifying ivy according to the leaf shapes with eight categories. This system has now been widely accepted and is being used by The American Ivy Society as well as in national flower shows. So, once again, the ivies selected for description in this book will be put into chapters according to the Pierot System of Ivy Classification.

If you are interested in ivy, I would urge you to join The American Ivy Society. The society, which started with only a handful of members, has become an important plant society with many chapters and a convention held annually in different parts of the United States or in England.

The American Ivy Society was selected by the International Committee on Horticultural Nomenclature and Registration to be the world-wide registration body for ivy nomenclature. Under the able direction of Dr. Sabina Mueller Sulgrove as registrar, the Society verifies that a new ivy "find" is indeed new, that the name conforms to accepted standards and that the "new" plant is not just an unstable "sport" of another ivy. The Society also conducts hardiness trials and has reference collections across the United States. For a list of addresses see Source List at the end of this book.

While among the members of the Society are the leading authorities on ivy, many are people who garden only on weekends and just want to know a little more about this versatile and adaptable plant. It is a happy friendly society. Membership is $15 and includes the Ivy Journal, 3 newsletters and a free Ivy plant every April. For more information, mail your name and address to:

The American Ivy Society
% Daphne Pfaff, Membership Chairman
696 Sixteenth Avenue South
Naples, Florida 33940

Acknowledgments

I NEVER thought 21 years ago when I wrote the first edition of The Ivy Book that the plant and the Society devoted to it would become such a big part of my life.

The American Ivy Society started with only a handful of members. Today it is a flourishing society with chapters across the nation, and a journal that is one of the most professionally produced in the country.

A great deal of the credit for the success of the Society goes to Patricia Riley Hammer, the President, Dr. Sabina Mueller Sulgrove, Registrar for Hedera, and to Rachel Cobb, Director of Publications.

For years Pat was in charge of the extraordinary topiaries created at Longwood Gardens in Kennett Square, Pennsylvania. Today she has her own business called "Samia Rose Topiary" in Encinitas, California (near San Diego). She is talented, artistic and devoted.

Rachel Cobb is a designer for one of the leading magazines in the United States. But she gives unstintingly of her time and energy to producing the Ivy Journal and the News Letters.

I don't know how to say thank you to Sabina Sulgrove. She has been a guiding rudder for the Society. There have been many times that members thought she was being too "picky" in her decision making about ivy nomenclature. But it is her very pickiness that has made her such a success as the world-wide Registrar for Hedera. She has been an enormous help to me in selecting the ivies chosen for this second edition, and for providing up-to-date information about them. Her skill as a photographer can be seen from the close-up photographs in this book. She is generous with her time, knowledge and friendship. I, personally, owe her an enormous debt of gratitude, and so does the society.

My life has changed radically since I wrote the first edition of this book. I became a widow. Again. Chance, or fate, took me to Costa Rica where I now live for almost half the year. Ivy grows perfectly well in the capital, San Jose, where the climate all year is much like San Diego, California. But where I live, deep in the jungle, it is hot and humid - and extremely beautiful. But Ivy doesn't like it there at all. So I now grow many different kinds of tropical flowers and leaves which I export to New York, Paris and Amsterdam. I also export coconuts around the world.

When I return home to Woodstock, New York - well after the winter is over - I am always so happy to see my faithful ivy plants waiting for me with all their new little shoots greeting the return of good weather.

To all my friends in The American Ivy Society, I say thank you. And a big thank you to Hedera itself.

Suzanne Warner Pierot
President Emerita
The American Ivy Society
Costa Rica, 1995

The Ivy Book

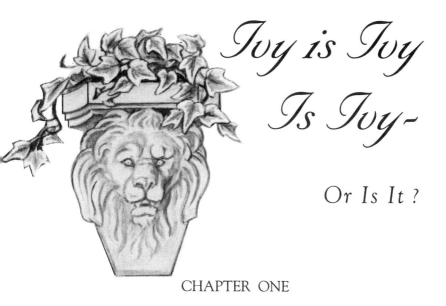

Ivy is Ivy Is Ivy-

Or Is It?

CHAPTER ONE

IVY IS the practical joker of the plant world. A gracefully elegant mischievous beauty of a plant that seems to delight in baffling the botanists in their efforts to straighten out the tangled nomenclature of its many forms. It's easy to tell that an ivy is an ivy. The trick is to know what *kind* of ivy it is. Even the acknowledged *experts* can't always agree on identification.

The problem of identifying the many kinds of ivy has been with us since Nero wore a wreath of it around his head, fiddling while Rome burned. The reason is simple: The only available clues are the shape, size, veins, and different colors of the leaves; and with only these clues, determination is difficult since older and younger leaves on the *same stem* may look different.

The problem is actually even more complicated. If three different people bought the same kind of ivy, on the same day, from the same nursery—six months later their plants could look like three different kinds of ivy because of the different environments they were put in and the different amounts of sunlight, water, and food they received. What's more, not one of the horticultural varieties of ivy grows true from seed. Adding to this botanical bewilderment is the carefree and very confusing way the ivy itself chooses to grow. You may have a beautiful, healthy, marvelous-looking ivy plant with all the leaves looking pretty much alike, then suddenly a new kind of leaf or shoot will show up. If you propagate that leaf or shoot, chances are you'll get an ivy that is completely different from the parent plant. Shoots such as these are called *sports*. Ivy's tendency to produce a shoot, or sport, with leaves different from the mother plant usually occurs when life has been good to the plant; it often happens in a greenhouse.

When a nurseryman sees a sport with an especially new and different kind of leaf shape, he is usually quick to propagate it. He gives the sport a new name, sends it all over the country, and then, more often than not, it "sports" back to one of its primitive forms. Many a sport has made "bad sports" of ivy fanciers because many of the trade names given to supposedly new discoveries are local names of the sports.

Compounding the confusion resulting from this impish ivy is the fact that there are several different kinds of sports. There is the *bud* sport, which comes from the tip of the juvenile foliage and is the rascal that refuses to produce the plant it came from when propagated from a cutting. Another is called the *intermediate* sport, which shoots up when the plant is between its adult and juvenile stage. These sports are the prolific ones, and each is different from the other.

Yet, as different as each ivy plant looks, all of them came from just six species. This intriguing fact makes ivy fun to grow and keep as a guest in your home or garden because there's never a dull moment with it.

And that's why so much space is devoted in this book to life-size, close-up photographs of as many ivies as possible. The ivy in this book is organized into eight categories:

Bird's Foot

Fans

Curlies

Heart Shapes

Variegateds or Multicolored

Miniatures

Ivy-Ivies

Oddities

Ivy's Shady History

CHAPTER TWO

IVY STARTED out as an emblem of virtue, prosperity and beneficence; but somewhere along the line it got mixed up with the licentious orgies of Bacchus. There is a happy ending: Like its habit of growing, ivy was able to rise above its surroundings and any bad reputation it ever had.

Ivy has been eulogized by poets (Horace, Vergil, Chaucer, Dryden, Dickens, et al.); glorified by artists (Wedgwood); symbolized by craftsmen (Hitchcock); etched in glass (Lalique); plasticized by merchants (Woolworth); and even embodied in academic form by college students (the Ivy League). No wonder the ivy has a sense of humor.

It isn't easy to trace ivy's historical growth with any degree of accuracy (and without laughing a lot), but it is known that one of the chief deities of Egypt, Osiris, who gave his people their knowledge of agriculture, adopted ivy as a symbol of his benefactions to mankind. Ivy in the Egyptian language was called *Chen-Osiris*, "the plant of Osiris". The ivy-wreathed thyrus, a long rod or wand, became the symbol of Osiris. But like everything else that starts out with noble motives, Osiris's rod became a lethal weapon in some situations. It was not unusual for someone to hid a spear under the ivy leaves and for the spear-bearer to take some unneighborly jabs at his neighbors.

Meanwhile, back in Greece, there was a god by the name of Dionysus. He was the Olympian god of nature (sometimes known as the God of the vine-or wine). In Rome the same god was called Bacchus. Bacchus had a great admiration for Osiris, and in an effort to honor him, he adopted the ivy for his own brand of worship. Some scholars have concluded that Bacchus's worship of ivy was because it reputedly modified the intoxicating effect of wine—a rather foolish and unrealistic conclusion, I think. Why would Bacchus and his followers, who liked nothing better than the juice of the grape, want to weaken its effect and slow down the orgies associated with it?

If you study the drawings and paintings of the bacchanalian feasts, you'll see many of the guests with wreaths or garlands of ivy draped around their heads. Maybe a little askew but, nevertheless on their heads.

Pliny the Elder, a Roman naturalist (A.D. 23-79), who made a study of the various kinds of ivies, claims that Bacchus was the first to use garlands and that ivy was the leaf that was used.

Vergil, in his fifth Pastoral, poetically reported that ivy was used even in the memorials to Bacchus. Daphnis, the shepherd, was not only a lover of some note, but according to Vergil:

> *Fierce tigers Daphis taught the yoke to bear;*
> *And first with curling ivy dressed the spear.*
> *Daphnis did rites to Bacchus first ordain;*
> *And holy revels for his reeling train.*

Ivy was a favorite with poets throughout the centuries, but it received scant biblical notice. Though not mentioned by name in the Bible, ivy formed "the corruptible crown" for which the athletes at the Isthmian games contended. Ivy is mentioned in the book of Maccabees:

And in the day of the king's birth, every month they were brought by bitter constraint to eat of the sacrifices; and when the feast of Bacchus was kept, the Jews were compelled to go in procession to Bacchus, carrying Ivy.

Ivy's historical background is as intriguing and varied as its method of growing. Ivy found its way into the Christian world; in their celebrations of Jesus' birth, the early Christians used ivy in their garlands. Even the old English carols gave ivy a place of honor:

> *Holly hat berys as red as any Rose*
> *The foster the huners, kepe hem from the doo,*
> > *Nay, Ivy! Nay, hyt, shall not.*

> *Ivy hat berys as black as any slo;*
> *There com the oule and ete him as she go.*
> > *Nay, Ivy! Nay, hyt, shall not.*

Though ivy did enjoy a modicum of respectability, it couldn't quite shake its association with Bacchus. Ivy was used in probably the very first sign made to advertise a saloon. "The sign of the bush" over a doorway, or even in front of a tent, meant that good cheer was available inside. The sign was a pole with a bunch of green leaves tied to the end of it, and the leaves were usually ivy. Chaucer called the pole an "alestake":

> A garland hadde he sette up on his hede
> As gret as it were for an alestake.

Most people called it an "alepole", and most inns used it as their only sign. The "alepole" or "alestake" often extended so far across the highway that riders struck their heads against them, until in 1375 an Act of Parliament restricted their length to seven feet. Eventually, the better bars adopted ivy in their names. "The Ivy Bush", "The Ivy Green", "Ivy Inn" were a few of them. As time went on and tastes improved (decorative tastes, that is), the more elegant bistros announced their goodies to the world by simply displaying a painting of Bacchus sitting on a cask with a wreath of ivy leaves around his head.

But it was the poets who gave ivy a place of honor. Horace, the lyric poet of his day (circa 65 B.C.), considered ivy worthy enough to be associated with his benefactor Maecenas:

> An ivy-wreath, fair learning's prize,
> Raises Maecenas to the skies.

Byron described ivy as "the garland of eternity." Wordsworth and Keats identified it with the majesty of maturity:

Grey locks profusely round his temples hung
In clustering curles, like ivy, which the bit
of winter cannot thin . . .
                    -"The Excursion," Wordsworth

His aged head, crown's with beechen wreath,
Seem'd like a poll of ivy in the teeth
Of Winter hoar.
                    "Endymion," Keats

Shakespeare mentioned ivy at least four times, but it was
Charles Dickens who wrote the most charming tribute in "The
Ivy Green":

Oh a dainty plant is the Ivy green,
        that creepeth o'er ruins old!
Of right choice food are his meals I ween,
        In his cell so lone and cold.
The wall must be crumbled, the stone decayed,
        To pleasure his dainty whim;
And the mouldering dust that years have made,
        Is a merry meal for him.
                Creeping where no life is seen,
                A rare old plant is the Ivy green.

Fast he stealeth on, though he wears no wings
        And a staunch old heart has he.
How closely he twineth, how tight he clings,
        to his friend the huge Oak Tree!

And slily he traileth along the ground,
  And his leaves he gently waves,
As he joyously hugs and crawleth round
    the rich mould of dead men's graves.
        Creeping where grim death is seen,
        A rare old plant is the Ivy green.

Whole ages have fled and their works decay'd,
  And nations have scatter'd been;
But the stout old Ivy shall never fade,
  From its hale and hearty green.
The brave old plant in its lonely days
  Shall fatten upon the past;
For the stateliest building man can raise
  Is the Ivy's food at last.
        Creeping on where time has been
        A rare old plant is the Ivy green.

Ivy has been accused of possessing the habits and vices of a vampire and living off the blood of aged and decrepit buildings. Yet, it has kept many a wall standing by absorbing the dampness that threatened to make the wall crumble and decay. I am convinced that many a stately home in England, and many a neglected medieval building, remains standing today because ivy chose centuries ago to throw a resplendent green mantle of glossy protection over it.

Of course, ivy does loosen mortar. It does get under clap-boards. It can be destructive and must be kept in check on some buildings. But, for instant age and that "old world" look, nothing surpasses it. All you need is the money for repairs.

I don't like to grow any climbing plant, be it ivy or a rambling rose, directly onto the wall of a house, particularly if it requires painting from time to time, because much of the plant is destroyed when it is pulled away from the wall. Instead, grow the plant on a trellis which is hinged at the bottom. When new paint is needed, lay the trellis down on the ground and cover with a plastic sheet. When the painting is finished just lift the trellis back into place. It is the hinge that does the trick.

Through the centuries there have been many people who have accused ivy of strangling trees in its determination to cover everything it touches. But ivy is not a parasite. Parasites do not produce green leaves or manufacture chlorophyll. The ivy does not sap the energies of a tree to live. It does not need the tree's nutriment. It certainly gets no nourishment from a stone wall; yet it thrives as much on a lifeless wall as it does on a tree.

Jefferson grew ivy at Monticello, but it was not a native plant. This was borne out by several books written in the eighteenth and nineteenth centuries and even in the writings of Captain John Smith (of Pocahontas fame) back in 1624. In "Virginia, the generalle historie of Virginia, New England and the Summer Isles," the good Captain wrote "The poysoned weed is much in shape like our English ivy."

In a book called *Travels in North America*, written by Peter Kalm and published in 1748, the author relates:

> *Near the town [Philadelphia], I saw an ivy or Hedera helix, planted against the wall of a stone building which was so covered by the fine green leaves of this plant as almost to conceal the whole. It was doubtless brought over from Europe for I have never perceived it anywhere else in my travels through North America.*

"A Treatise on the Theory and Practice of Landscape Gardening adapted to North America" written by Andrew Jackson Downing and published by Wiley and Putman (New York) in 1844, states:

> *The Ivy is not a native of America; nor is it by any means a very common plant in our gardens, though we know of no apology for the apparent neglect of so beautiful a climber . . . One of the most beautiful growths of this plant, which has ever met our eyes, is that upon the old mansion in the Botanic Garden at Philadelphia. . . .*

It was in the 1870s, shortly after the Civil War, that ivy got a firm hold in the United States. Ocean travel for many Americans was becoming popular, and outdoor photography was coming into its own. Travelers returning from England brought back many pictures of ivy-covered buildings, especially castles and old manor houses. In American, ivy was so treasured that it was grown in pots and used as a living frame around doorways, windows, mirrors, and paintings. A big fad was indoor screens completely covered with growing ivy. Soon it became the favorite decorating motif for furniture, dinnerware, glassware, wallpaper, and many objets d'art. It still is.

A person can go to Tiffany's in New York and buy an ivy-decorated dinner plate made by Wedgwood for about fifteen or twenty dollars and then walk down the street to the first five-and-ten-cent store and find the same design on a plastic ruffle for shelf edging.

From Bacchus to Woolworth, ivy has had quite a life.

Ivy Culture

or All That's Needed
Is a Little Love

CHAPTER THREE

HOW MANY time have you visited a well-kept, attractive home and noticed a pitiful ivy in a pot struggling for its life? Sure, it has leaves. And they're green. But the wide gaps where leaves once flourished are mute testimony to sad neglect.

If you do what no nice guest would do and peek into the pot, you'd probably find the soil dry and parched, cracked and crumbling. If your hostess, who probably spends hours every week fussing with her hair or nails, had devoted just a few minutes of attention to her potted friend, she could have been rewarded with a green, lush, fully leafed oasis of gracefulness.

It's so easy to turn ivy into an exciting showpiece that your friends can ooh and ahh over when they see it in your home. Not much needs to be done. You need to observe only a few simple rules to steer that middle course between coddling and utter neglect. That's one of the joys of raising ivy.

Soil

Ivy isn't fussy about soil as long as it has good drainage. Of course, a rich, organic soil will produce faster and thicker growth, but it isn't vital. In fact, variegated ivies should be grown in poor soil to stimulate the growth of colored foliage. If you give the variegateds too much food, the leaves will be mainly green.

To get good drainage in ordinary soil, mix a little perlite in it. Perlite is probably one of the greatest soil aids ever created. The little white granules are pretty, too. You may also mix a little vermiculite in the soil. Many people find that vermiculite retains too much water, especially when watering is done with a heavy hand. Vermiculite is acceptable if you're not a compulsive waterer.

Peat moss and milled sphagnum are also excellent soil additives. The important thing is that whatever the soil, you must keep it moist-not soggy.

Many people have the erroneous impression that ivy requires a very acid soils - not so. A pH of 6.0 to 7.0 is ideal, and unless your soil comes from the deep woods (where it is very acid) or if you happen to live on a limestone rock (which is alkaline), chances are your soil is absolutely perfect for ivy. If you want to be really accurate and have fun too, you can buy a soil-testing kit at any garden-supply store. These kits are inexpensive and easy to use.

What does pH mean? It's really quite simple. A soil's pH is a measurement of its *hydrogen ion concentration*. The pH scale reads from 1 to 14. 7 is neutral and readings above that point mean that the soil is alkaline. For instance, if your soil has a pH 7.8 you may be sure it is on the alkaline side. The higher the number is above 7, such as pH 7.8 or 8.0, the greater the alkalinity of your soil. If the figure is below 7, the soil will tend to be acid. The lower the number is below 7, such as pH 6.5, 6.0, or 5.0, the higher the acidity of your soil.

The most satisfactory pH for a garden soil in which many different plants can be grown (including ivy) is between pH 6.5 and pH 7.0. A pH 8.0 shows signs of severe mineral deficiency and would starve your plants. The soil should be carefully fed until the requisite pH is acquired.

When growing ivy outdoors, simply make sure the soil is good garden loam with adequate drainage. To get professional help at no cost, send a sample of your soil in a small plastic bag to the Agricultural Extension Station in your state.

Fertilizer

For indoor ivy any "balanced" fertilizer such as 10-10-10- or 15-15-15- is excellent. A fertilizer is balanced when the three numbers in the formula are the same. Those three numbers stand for the amount of nitrogen, phosphoric acid, and potash in the formula, and in that order. (An unbalanced fertilizer, such as 15-30-15, is used for flowering plants.)

There are many good brands of fertilizer on the market such as Peters, Rapid-Gro, and Mircle-Gro. All these brands indicate their formula on the label.

Unless they are variegated ivies, fertilize your plants every other week, or at least once a month. I remind myself on the first and fifteenth of the month that it is fertilizer time, but if you should miss a date, don't worry. Ivy is always grateful for any kindness bestowed on it and forgives an occasional lapse.

When ivy is used as a ground cover, plant it in a well-prepared soil, mulched with hay to prevent washing-out and weed growth. Space plants one foot apart in each direction. In this case, you can lime, if necessary, and fertilize the soil before applying the hay.

In establishing the ground-cover planting, two fertilizations, one at time of planting and another two months later, are desirable. Usually two to three pounds of 10-10-10 fertilizer per 100 square feet is ideal. Once this is established, fertilize infrequently because over stimulation tends to soften the stems and make the plants susceptible to winter kill.

When fertilizing topiaries, it is a good idea to put liquid fertilizer in a spray bottle and spray directly on the leaves, in addition to pouring it onto the soil.

Watering

The most important aspect of caring for ivy is the simplest — watering. Ivy thrives in moist soil. *Moist*, I said, not soggy. If you want to show your ivy the absolute in affection, you will put it in the sink once in a while and give it a brisk shower. This not only keeps the leaves clean and shiny, but it will also help get rid of any spider mites that might be lurking underneath the leaves.

If you have a grafted plant lay the plant on its side and spray; don't set it erect until all excess water has drained from it. The weight of the top growth plus the added weight of the excess water can be enough to pull the grafts right out of their sockets.

Ivy would rather be kept in a humid room. If you don't care to live that way, simply set the plant on a tray with wet pebbles or damp peat moss and your ivy will be perfectly content.

It is remarkable how many novices believe that ivy should be kept soaking wet. Possibly this is because cut vines of almost any ivy root readily and grown in water, however ivy in a pot will not tolerate a soggy soil. Good drainage and a humid atmosphere are its beauty secrets.

The eminent horticulturalist Alfred Bates related an interesting story of his experience with watering:

> *The first thing I found out about the nature of the Ivy was the very great difference that the amount of moisture in the soil had upon it; causing so great an increase in the size of the leaf and in the distance between nodes as to completely change the appearance of the plant. Years ago three cuttings were got from a very small leaved, dark green variety of which I am still uncertain as to the name; after they were rooted one was planted in almost full shade where the ground was only comparatively moist, the second was planted below a low stone edging in almost full sun but where water stood for some time after every rain and the third was grown in a pot where it was given regular and copious watering.*

*The last two grew luxuriously until they approached the variety gracilis both in leaf and inter-node while the first, that in the drier soil, has still retained its small leaf and its rather short inter-node. It has slowly climbed up an old grape arbor post until now that it has reached the top and is beginning to send out stems which search for more support I hope that I may be able to obtained it in an arborescent form."**

When ivy is being trained to grow either as a topiary or on some kind of wire form it must be sprayed regularly with water. Ivy is a most agreeable plant, but if you are making it into a showpiece topiary you are also transforming it into a prima donna. You must therefore treat it like a prima donna and spray it at least once a day, preferably twice.

The Bronx Sprayer (available at garden-supply centers) is probably one of the best of all sprayers. However if you are inclined to be lazy, as well as economical, save all your hair-setting-lotion bottles or any detergent bottle that comes with a spray top. (Get-set, Windex, Fantastic, to name a few.) Leave one next to each topiary, and then whenever you pass by, it will be easy to give the plant a little spraying.

Larger topiaries, such as a 3-foot-tall flamingo I once made, demand about a gallon of water daily. The flamingo sat beside my water-lily pool and every time I passed it, I poured the entire watering can over it. The water drippings fell into the pool. That's something to remember when you bring your topiaries into the house for the winter. Place them were drippings won't do any damage, or be prepare to mop.

*Alfred Bates, "The Illusive Ivy," *National Horticulture Magazine,* January 1932.

$\mathcal{L}$ight

Ivies will tolerate far more sun than most people realize, except that under full sunlight they grow considerably slower. Ivy, by nature, is a shade-loving plant, but it certainly will grow in full sun. What is dangerous about planting it in full sun is that the winter sun will do more harm to it than the winter cold. Except for the tender species, ivies take more kindly to frost or a light freeze than they do to the dry heat of a room or the harsh rays of a winter sun.

$\mathcal{P}$lanting $\mathcal{I}$nstructions

The secret to successful gardening with ivies is to plant them deep into the ground. Remove the lowest 2-4 leaves - or even half the leaves of the above-ground portion. Bury the root ball straight into the ground up to the leaf stalk of the now - lowest leaf. This allows the plant to form new stems and roots along the bare portion of the sunken stem, and thus anchor the plant more firmly in the ground. The deeper the roots are in the ground, the less chance of scorching from drought or frost-heaving in winter. It takes about three years for root systems of any plant to become well established. For best results chooses a location out of late afternoon sun.

Diseases and Insects

Ivy doesn't usually tell you it's sick. So, if you don't give it a checkup once in a while, you'll never know until it's too late. Many problems will be avoided by regularly washing leaves.

SCALE:
Every so often, lift a few leaves and look for scattered brown bumps stuck underneath. If you see any, it means your ivy has scale. These insects are almost invisible, and that's when they're doing the most damage. It is not until they form their hard scale-like shell that they are visible. Spray over and under leaves with Malathion, mixed according to package directions.

MITES:
Mites are common on ivy, especially during hot and dry seasons or if kept in a moistureless room. These pests are hard to see without a magnifying glass, but their damage resembles tiny, grey needle-like specks on the leaves. Spray with Malathion or Kelthane.

RED SPIDER:

These are tiny eight-legged mites that live on the underside of leaves and can be seen with a hand lens. They suck the sap of the leaf and cause speckling and discoloration of the leaves. Spray with Malathion or Blackleaf 40.

LEAF SPOT:

Ivy can get leaf spot and aphids, although neither are common. Leaf spot causes one-quarter-inch brown spots that appear on the underside of the leaf and often come through to the top. If you should see it, pick off and burn damaged leaves. Ivy grown in full sun where heat is intense is more susceptible to leaf spot. Spray with a fungicide containing copper or use Bordeaux Mixture.

APHIDS:

Aphids, as you probably know, are soft-bodied, tiny insects that suck sap from the plant. Spray with Malathion or Lindane.

ANTHRACNOSE:

Symptoms of Anthracnose are black spots on the leaf and stem. Spray with a fungicide containing copper or use Bordeaux Mixture.

Propagation

Outdoors or indoors, ivy is a joy to propagate. When I lived in Stamford, Connecticut, I had a stone retaining wall around an island in the middle of the Rippowam River. The wall looked bare, and I wanted it softened with the gracefulness of ivy. Instead of making a lot of little cuttings, I pulled the long strands from some ivy I had growing in abundance in another section of the garden. The strands that had a root at one end must have been at least twenty feet long.

I simply planted the root and laid the full twenty feet in the soil along the edge of the wall. I planted one strand after the other until the wall was encircled. Then, between each cluster of leaves, I covered the vine with soil. It wasn't long before each cluster of leaves had become a new plant of ivy and magnificently cascaded over the wall into the river.

Often, long strands of ivy trailing on the ground root themselves this way naturally. This is called *layering*. To make cuttings from layered plants, cut off vines where they have rooted and replant.

You can also take tip cuttings by snipping the ends of trailing vines and putting them in water. Remove any leaves that would be covered with water. In a short time these plants will have sufficient roots for use in containers of water. Ivy that is rooted in water does not transplant well into soil. If you want to grow them in soil, root your cuttings in moist vermiculite mixed with sand or perlite for drainage.

To root cuttings, remove the bottom leaf or leaves and insert the cuttings in rows in a flat or pot of vermiculite and sand, or a mixture of vermiculite and perlite. Keep the flat or pot moist and shaded until fresh new leaves form, which indicates that the roots are growing and have taken hold. Another way is to give a gentle tug to the cutting - very gentle - and if there is a little resistance, you'll know the roots have formed.

The Nitty Gritty About Ivy

Or The Botanist's Eye-view of Hedera

CHAPTER FOUR

THE PURPOSE of this book is to help you understand a rather complex plant in a simple and agreeable manner. If you are interested in delving a little deeper into the peculiarities of ivy, this chapter should serve that purpose. On the other hand, if diagnosing variants and probing foliage differences is not your cup of tea, then you may just as well skip this chapter. All the information you need for identifying the myriad ivy varieties as well as growing beautiful lush plants and topiaries is in the chapters ahead.

Ivy's botanical name is *Hedera* (hed'-er'a), and it belongs to the *Araliaceae* family. *Hedera* is its classical name, and the origin is Latin. Ivy is described by botanists as a climbing or ascendent woody plant that becomes shrublike or treeform at maturity. The two steps are, for the most part, distinct. In their juvenile stage of development all ivies have climbing stems supported by aerial rootlets that are present in varying degrees of abundance. At this stage the plants do not flower. In the adult stage, when the plant becomes shrubby, the ivy has no aerial rootlets, and the climbing tendency disappears. It flowers and bears fruit. But, with the exception of "238th Street," this rarely happens in the colder northern climates.

The juvenile stage has ended and the adult stage has begun when you find an erect ascending branch without aerial rootlets and with unfamiliar foliage. It is on these branches that the flower and fruits are borne. These fruits, which look like little berries, are poisonous.

Juvenile leaves on the same plant can have an entirely different shape and size than the adult leaves, or from each other. They can even have a different number of lobes or no lobes at all. The younger leaves are of lighter color than the older leaves, but don't be surprised to find that some of the older leaves are smaller than some of the younger.

It is almost impossible to tell the variety the adult leaves originated from if the cutting is taken away from the plant. Botanists can identify species of ivy by the character of "hairs" on the lowerside of the foliage and on the stalks of the fruit, which are so small one needs a strong magnifying lens to see them and a microscope to identify them.

There are six species of Hedera in cultivation, and they can be identified most easily in their juvenile stage. The ivy most often grown is Hedera helix and there are over 400 varieties grown in the United States. The other five species have only a few varieties. The six species are:

> Hedera helix
> Hedera canariensis
> Hedera rhombea
> Hedera colchica
> Hedera nepalensis
> Hedera pastuchovii

Hedera Helix: English Ivy

This is the species you find most frequently in America and Western Europe, both cultivated and naturalized. (The English prefer to call it "The Ivy.") It is hardy in most parts of the United States. Two of the most popular outdoor varieties are hibernica and baltica, and of these two varieties, baltica is probably the most hardy.

The varieties and clones of *Hedera helix* can be distinguished by their juvenile foliage, which is dark green and has whitish veins. The leathery leaves are from one to three inches long or longer, usually five-lobed with heart-shaped bases. The hairs seen through a microscope, have four to six rays. Stems are dull green to purplish.

In the adult stage the foliage is uniformly olive-green without the whitish veins. The flowers are greenish yellow, the fruit black or yellowish orange. Clones of *Hedera helix* number in the hundreds. Fortunately they fall into three groups.

Group one: The self-branching ivies. This group produces an abundance of lateral branches along the stems in the leaf axils. Included in this group are 'Fan', 'Duck Foot', 'Manda Crested', and 'Ritterkreuz'.

Group two: These are ivies that are long and trailing and do not branch profusely, although some varieties may have an occasional lateral branch. Helix in group two include 'Erecta', 'Conglomerata', 'Curlilocks', 'Buttercup', 'Gold Heart', baltica*, and hibernica*

Group three: The variegated ivies. These are in a separate group because of their coloring, but their growing habit can be either self-branching or long and trailing. They include 'Goldust,' 'Green Quartz,' 'Goldheart', and 'Heise Denmark'.

Less is known about the origins of group two than about the other two groups. Groups one and three have been known for more than a century. Most of them are of British origin.

* These are botanical varieties, and although propagated as clones they can be found in the wild. The variety baltica is known as Baltic Ivy. Hibernica is known as Irish Ivy.

Hedera Canariensis:
Canary Island Ivy

This species, the darling of the florists, is a native of North Africa and is grown outdoors all over the West Coast of the United States. Most of the large-leafed variegated ivies belong to this species, and while they are not reliably hardy outdoors, except on the West Coast and in the South, they do make spectacular house plants. An ivy expert, Mrs. Arthur Michaels of Rye, New York, grows her *Hedera canariensis* in a protected spot under a covering of pine needles that fall naturally from the trees above. I would be afraid to grow it farther north than southern Connecticut.

Hedera Canariensis is the only ivy species that produces bright burgundy-red twigs and leaf stems. Its leaves are large (seven or eight inches across) glossy, and more apple-green in color than you find in the other species. Its hairs are grayish white with about fifteen rays, which tend occasionally to be star shaped. Juvenile leaves commence egg shaped, then become triangular and unlobed. During growth they develop from three to five lobes. In the adult stage (depending on the climate, it can take many years) the leaves become egg shaped again although slightly thicker and less glossy than in their juvenile stage. Its fruit is black and the size of a pea. Varieties of *Hedera canariensis* include 'Canary Cream,' 'Variegata,' and 'Margino-maculata'.

Hedera Colchica: Persian Ivy

A native of most of Asia and Southeastern Europe, *Hedera colchica* can be fairly easily identified by its rather thick, leathery, heart-shaped, pointed leaves and dull, dark green color. Crush the leaves and they smell like celery! The stems are a pea-green and very scaly. *Colchica's* hair is yellow with about eighteen to thirty rays. The leaves of the juvenile foliage are broadly egg shaped and occasionally three-lobed. On the lowerside of the leaves the surface is ribbed. The veins on the upperside of the leaf are ribbed near the base and gradually become depressed across the rest of the surface. The adult foliage does not differ from the juvenile foliage to any great extent except that it is narrower and, of course, the leaves do not have any lobes. *Hedera colchica's* pea-sized fruit is blue black at maturity. Some of the varieties are 'Dentata,' and 'Dentato-variegata'.

Hedera Nepalensis: Nepal Ivy

As you might expect, this species is native to Nepal and grows not only in India but throughout Southeast Asia. It was discovered by N. Wallich in 1824. In its juvenile stage it can be identified by its narrow, tapering leaves, which are a dull green color mottled with areas of gray green. There are between two and four narrow lobes on each side of the leaf, although young leaves do not always show this lobing. The hairs are scaly, more often twelve to fifteen rays and yellowish brown. The hairs are abundant on the stems, infrequent on juvenile foliage, and absent on mature leaves. The adult leaves are narrow and tapering, unlobed, and have a wavy form. The fruit is fairly large and is orange in color.

In the first edition of this book I said that I did not have *Hedera nepalensis* in my collection. Shortly thereafter I was deeply honored when Dr. John Creech of the U. S. National Arboretum named one that he discovered in Nepal, 'Suzanne', and presented me with several plants. I had also been told by friends that it is not hardy in northern regions of the United States.

However, I now live in Woodstock, New York (Zone 5) and have grown 'Suzanne' outdoors in a protected spot for several years.

Hedera Rhombea: Japanese Ivy

This ivy species grows all over Japan except in the most northern regions. Its juvenile leaves are three-to-five-lobed, and they are egg shaped. Its veins are depressed. It is graceful and has a wider range of color than most other ivies. *Hedera rhombea's* hairs are grayish brown and scaly with seven to fourteen rays. In the adult stage the leaves are unlobed, narrow, and tapering in form. It is not reliably hardy, and so it should be grown outdoors or in a cold frame.

There is a variegated clone called 'Variegata' whose leaves are bright green with a narrow white border around them.

'Pierot' is all green and has a delicate form of growth. It is reputed to be not reliably hardy, but I am growing it also in Zone 5. I cover it in the winter with a mulch of pine needles.

Hedera Pastuchovii: Russian Ivy

This ivy was first collected in Russia and later from the Caspian Forest area of Iran. The leaves are long, narrow and unlobed with a blue-green glossy hue. It is a great climber and clings without much help.

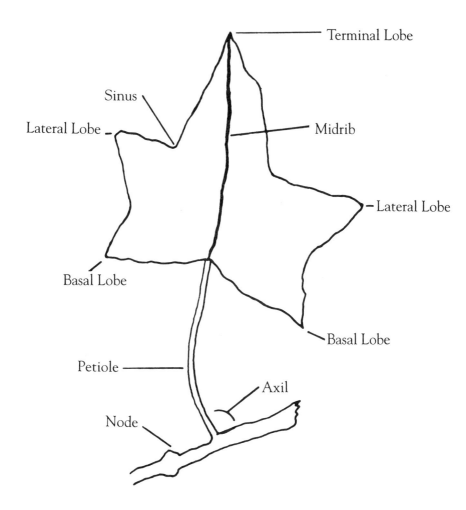

Terminal Lobe

Sinus

Midrib

Lateral Lobe

Lateral Lobe

Basal Lobe

Basal Lobe

Petiole

Axil

Node

Ivy Terms Made Easy

Midrib   The rib that runs vertically from petiole to the top of the terminal lobe.

Lobe   A projection of a leaf regardless of shape.

Terminal Lobe   The projection at the top of leaf.

Lateral Lobes   The projections at the side of leaf. It is found on leaves with five lobes or more.

Basal Lobes   The projections found at base of leaf. The basal lobes are sometimes so small they go almost unnoticed.

Petiole   The supporting stalk or stem of a leaf.

Sinus   The angle or curve between two lobes.

Axil   The angle between the petiole and the vine.

Node   The joint of the vine where a petiole grows.

Classification

The Pierot Classification System

(As Amplified by The American Ivy Society)

CHAPTER FIVE

Note: Cultivars may fall into more than one category.

Bird's Foot   Leaves with narrow lobes resembling a bird's track in the snow. Example 'Needlepoint', 'Pedata'.

Fans   Leaves very broad and fan-shaped with lobes of equal length ('Fan'), or the lobes of unequal length but all forward-pointing and the veins prominently raised above the leaf surface ('Triton').

Curlies	Leaves with ruffles, ripples or pleats involving the entire leaf or with a significant rippling of the margin. Example 'Telecurl'.
Variegateds	Multi-colored leaves of shades of green and gray with white, yellow, or light green markings. Examples: 'Glacier', 'Gold Child'.

The intensity and the patterns of colors may vary with light levels and temperatures, or the variegation may change with the maturation of the leaf ('Buttercup').

Multi-color variegations may also be classified by pattern, such as an all-over pattern as in 'Gold Dust' or central variegation ('Gold Heart').

Color - other than green - may also occur in Ivy, but is not considered as variegation in the strict sense. Stems may also be pink or maroon instead of green. Leaves may show winter colors of pink to red, maroon and purple. Example: 'Gold Heart'.

Heart-shaped	Leaves heart-shaped or shield-shaped ('Deltoidea') including triangular three-lobed leaves with sharp or rounded lobes ('Garland').

Miniature   Leaves less than one inch long of any shape. The plants are also delicate or refined in appearance. Example: 'Duck Foot', 'Midget'.

Ivy-Ivies   Typical ivy leaves, almost flat, palmately lobed, with five lobes-a pronounced terminal lateral, and recognizable basal lobes. Example: 'Pittsburgh'.

Oddities   Plants of unusual form, such as upright or non-vining ('Congesta') or plants that have fasciated, asymmetrical or distorted leaves ('Small Deal').

Bird's Foot Ivies

CHAPTER SIX

THIS GROUP of ivy is easily identified. If you've ever seen the track of a bird's foot in sand, then you'll be quick to spot this most interesting ivy. The resemblance to a bird's foot is most obvious in the miniatures of this group, particularly in 'Irish Lace'. In all varieties, the terminal lobe on each leaf is long and thin and the lateral lobes spread out almost making right angles.

Hedera Helix 'Pedata'

This indoor-outdoor climber has a dainty leaf and a tidy habit of growing that makes it marvelous for hanging baskets, in flower arrangements, on walls, and as a ground cover. Another delightful use of this ivy is to plant it inside a kitchen window as the Victorians used to do. Some of the vines can be trained to go up and across the window frame and down the other side, which makes quite a charming sight that may be enjoyed all year round.

SIZE AND SHAPE: *Hedera helix* 'Pedata' consists of leaves divided into five lobes with the middle lobe long and thin. The sinuses between the terminal and lateral lobes are very broad. Occasionally, you will find one or two slight protrusions of the sides of the terminal lobe. The basal lobes point backward like the heel of a bird's foot. Typical plants have leaves about one and one half inches long, but they vary and you may find them as small as one inch and as large as three inches.

COLOR: The leaves start life as a bright apple-green and become progressively darker as they mature until they are almost gray-green. The veins are silvery and raised, accentuating the footlike appearance of the leaf.

HABIT OF GROWTH: Because it is a fast grower with a graceful vining habit, be careful where you put each plant because the long vines will quickly find their way into places they don't belong. However, 'Pedata's' fast-growing habit can be used to great advantage when you need something covered fast. Try it over a trellis or on a split rail fence. Prune it back occasionally.

CULTURE: It will grow equally well in sun or shade, but the nodes will be more widely spaced if grown in the shade. Try layering this variety. Take the longest vines and attach them to the ground with a heavy wire or hair pin. They should root quickly.

Hedera Helix 'Shamrock'

One of the prettiest topiaries I ever saw was a "poodle" made with 'Shamrock'. It looked almost real enough to bark, and it won a "first" at the International Flower Show in New York City for Mrs. Colby Chester of Greenwich, Connecticut.

'Shamrock' is unusual and a fast grower. It is not only good for topiaries, but also for flower arrangements and table decoration.

Where it got its name causes some controversy. In Europe it is sometimes called 'Cloverleaf' ivy. It was introduced to the florist trade in the United Stated in 1957 at a meeting at the Shamrock Hotel in Houston, Texas and later patented in 1964.

SIZE AND SHAPE: The variety in the size of the leaves on this plant is astonishing. Some are tiny enough to resemble miniatures while others are an inch or two long. And they are all on the *same* vine. 'Shamrock' has a tendency to grow many leaves from one axil, which gives it a clustered look. An extra advantage is its self-branching quality. All this plus the fact that the leaves lie flat makes this ivy ideal for topiaries.

The leaf has five lobes, but the terminal and two lateral lobes are so equal in size that the leaf seems three-lobed. Because the sinuses are so deeply cut, each leaf appears to be three leaves clustered together. On some older leaves, the side lobes fold forward against the terminal lobe giving the leaf a layered look. It's really a great plant to study and is full of surprises.

COLOR: The leaves are dark green with light green veins.

HABIT OF GROWTH: Its habit of growth is one of its real assets. If you want a lovely, long trailing vine, 'Shamrock' has it. If you want lots of leaves for a fuller effect, 'Shamrock' will provide you with it. The leaf surface, especially on older leaves, may be slightly quilted or unevenly puckered, that is the light-green veins are sunken and the tissue in between is unevenly inflated.

CULTURE: Apparently the uniformity of the leaves on a vine - or conversely, the diversity of leaf sizes and the degree of fusion of the leaflets, from three separate leaflets to fused half-way at the base - is a function of the environmental growing conditions.

I find it will withstand more sunshine that most ivies. Because of its overlapping habit, a frequent thorough spraying with water will do it a world of good.

Hedera Helix 'Star'

I think you'll like this one immensely. Its habit of growth is beautiful, and its leaves look like the top half of a star. "Star' can be used in most topiaries, but don't use it where you would need sharp definition such as in an animal form. It would look marvelous in a ring, spiral, or geometric form. In the summer, grow it in an outdoor container with red, white and blue petunias. The sight is spectacular.

SIZE AND SHAPE: Although its lobes are slender, the leaves are certainly broader than most Bird's Foot ivies. Compare it with 'Irish Lace' and you'll quickly see how much broader it is. But a Bird's Foot it is, with long lobes and deeply cut sinuses. There are five lobes on each leaf, and each one is sharply pointed. The leaves vary from one inch to one and one half inches.

COLOR: 'Star' has a healthy grass-green color that is lovely. The veins have practically the same color as the leaves, and the vines are reddish.

HABIT OF GROWTH: It is supposed to be self-branching, and it is from time to time, but I have found that if you want to have a really full plant, it should be cut back. However, the long vines are so graceful as they twist and turn to reveal their star-like leaves that you may want to let the plant grow the way it wants to.

CULTURE: 'Star' does well in partial sunshine. It is not reliably hardy in colder climates unless you plant it deep and give it winter protection.

Hedera Helix 'Irish Lace'

My favorite by far of all the Bird's Foot ivies is 'Irish Lace'. It is the darling of the topiary fanciers and excels as an indoor plant. For a unique arrangement put a little soil into a large conch or decorative seashell and plant 'Irish Lace' in it. The effect makes quite a conversation piece.

SIZE AND SHAPE: This is the true Bird's Foot ivy. While the others remind you of a bird's foot, 'Irish Lace' *looks* like one with its delicate, long, thin five-lobed leaves. They are truly extraordinary in shape. Some of the lobes are over an inch long and only an eighth of an inch wide. Absolutely lovely.

COLOR: A rich, alive, dark green with lighter green veins.

HABIT OF GROWTH: Though its vines grow long, they are generously leafed - sometimes with as many as five leaves growing out from a single node. This gives each long strand a full, bushy appearance. there is only one imperfection to this otherwise perfect ivy variety. Occasionally the leaf shape, which makes the plant so unique, loses its thin, spindly appearance and grows into a broader leaf resembling 'Pedata'. I generally pick off those leaves.

CULTURE: It thrives on love and care. Spray it regularly. Better yet, if it is a pot plant, take the pot to the sink and wash all the leaves. Out doors plant it deeply and give winter protection. See page 21.

Hedera Helix 'Needlepoint'

'Needlepoint' is another dainty, perfectly shaped Bird's Foot that is very much like 'Irish Lace'.

SIZE AND SHAPE: The leaves of 'Needlepoint' are lighter green than those of 'Irish Lace'. To tell the difference between 'Irish Lace' and 'Needlepoint' feel the edges of the leaf. In 'Irish Lace' they are slightly rolled under, in 'Needlepoint, they are not.

COLOR: Bright dark green.

HABIT OF GROWTH: 'Needlepoint' is readily self-branching with short internodes and petioles.

CULTURE: Hardy to zone 4. Be sure to plant deep and give winter protection for at least three years. See page 21.

Hedera Helix 'Ritterkreuz'

The famed Longwood Gardens in Pennsylvania had a test garden for Ivies with about 100 different cultivars growing side-by-side each in its own little section. One of the spectacular successes of this test was 'Ritterkreuz'. So much so that when members of the Ivy Society would walk by they would chant - "Ok - let's hear it for 'Ritterkreuz' and a big cheer would go up". (Society members do incline to be enthusiastic!)

But this enthusiasm is warranted. The plant is lush, beautiful, and robust. It was discovered and registered by Ingobert Heick, the Brother in Charge of the Newburg Monastery Nursery in Heidelburg, Germany. 'Ritterkreuz' is a German word which translates into "knight's cross" or Maltese Cross, the emblem used by an order of knights of the Middle ages.

SIZE AND SHAPE: It has five sharply pointed lobes which are broad in the middle and constricted at the base - more or less diamond shaped with two small basal lobes appearing as teeth. The lobes are generally broader in the middle than 'Needlepoint'. Some people think it looks like a cut-leaf Maple. Leaves are one inch to one and one half inches.

COLOR: Dark green.

HABIT OF GROWTH: 'Ritterkreuz' is a sport of 'Needlepoint' and seems to be hardier. It is not noticeably self-branching. Fast grower.

CULTURE: Plant deeply. If need be, take off a few leaves from the bottom of stem to get the cutting or plant at least 3 or 4 inches deep into the soil. Semi-shade.

The Fans

CHAPTER SEVEN

THE FAN-SHAPED ivies are unique, with very broad leaves, some of which are reminiscent of the fans carried by the Ziegfeld girls, the beauties of the Roaring Twenties, and some look like fat chubby hands. The leaves generally have five to nine lobes of equal length and are easy to identify.

The fans are all very graceful, and none of them has that coarse leathery look found in so many ivies. I give my fans a prominent position in my home because they are so different looking and certainly not the usual variety of either house plant or ivy.

Fans do very well under electric light and can be placed on coffee or end tables to garner the attention they deserve. But, of course, that means more care on your part-more watering and showering.

Hedera Helix 'California Fan'

This plant is lush enough and has such a compact habit of growth that you may be forgiven for not recognizing it as an ivy. Of all the fan-shaped ivies, this is my favorite. I am particularly fascinated by the young leaves that start life with almost no indication of a lateral or basal lobe but are rather like little fingers stretching out from a plump little palm. Because this ivy is so compact and slow to trail, it makes a marvelous plant for a table top.

SIZE AND SHAPE: This ivy can have from five to nine lobes. (I have a plant with five-, seven-, and nine-lobed leaves *all* on the same vine.) The leaves range in size from one and one-half to two inches. Even in their fully grown state, the leaves are broader than they are long, and the lobes are short and abruptly acute. 'California Fan' reminds me a little of another fan, 'Old Garden', and it's easy to confuse one with the other.

COLOR: The young leaves have an alive apple-green appearance. The older leaves are a midsummer grass-green. The midrib is pronounced and the small veins radiating from it form a beautiful, intricate pattern. When examined closely, each leaf looks like a mosaic.

HABIT OF GROWTH: Compact and generous with leaves, 'California Fan' has a tendency to branch from the base with more than one leaf growing from each node.

CULTURE. Hardy to zone 4. Plant deeply. See page 21.

Hedera Helix 'Green Ripple'

I'm including 'Green Ripple' with Fans because it fits the group. But if you study it carefully, you'll find it is also much like the Bird's Foot ivies. It can be best described as a cross between the two. Its leaves are flat and broad like the Fans, but their long terminal lobes are much like the Bird's Foot.

SIZE AND SHAPE: The distinguishing feature of 'Green Ripple' is the size and length of the basal lobes on some of the leaves. The basal lobe is quite long, extending half-way up the leaf, which makes it look longer than it looks wide. But this occurs on only some of the leaves. Adding to the confusion is the fact that not all the leaves on the same vine are alike. Some have rounded basal lobes, giving the leaf a wide appearance.

On all leaves, however, a little pleat forms between the terminal and lateral lobes. Occasionally you'll also find a pleat between the lateral and basal lobe. These give the leaves a hint of a rippled look. The medium-size leaves grow from one inch to two and one-half inches. The majority of the leaves on my own plants seem to be longer than they are broad.

HABIT OF GROWTH: It is generous in its growth. Occasionally you'll find clusters of leaves coming from the axils. As the vine gets older it seems to lose this habit of growth, and so if you want a full bushy plant, keep it trimmed back. However, when not cut back, the leaves on the long trailing vines are very gracefully arranged and give a flowing effect.

CULTURE: Hardy to zone 4, if planted deeply. See page 21.

Hedera Helix 'Fan'

It is not easy to distinguish one Fan from another. The leaves of all Fans are broader than they are long, and this is markedly true with 'Fan'.

SIZE AND SHAPE: The five to seven short, fat-lobed leaves have shallow sinuses that form a pleat or wave. The older leaves are about two inches wide and about one and one half inches from the tip of the petiole to the tip of the terminal lobe. The young leaves are about three quarters of an inch long and one inch wide.

COLOR: A very delicate pastel green describes this plant. In most ivies the older leaves turn a darker green, but 'Fan' keeps the color of its youth. The veins are raised and very pronounced. The veins in the older leaves take on a whitish color.

HABIT OF GROWTH: A nice vining habit with the leaves staggered along the stem makes each vine look quite bushy. 'Fan' doesn't grow very fast, and so you won't have much need to cut it back. When it does get long enough, don't fail to make a cutting to plant next to the mother plant for a fuller, more bushy look. Another way to get a fuller look is to layer the ivy. See page 24.

CULTURE: Hardy to zone 4 if planted deeply and given winter protection.

Hedera Helix 'Pixie'

This is a beautiful example of ivy showing its sense of humor. Maybe that's why this plant is called 'Pixie'. Its leaves are a cross between a Bird's Foot and a Fan. The effect is interesting and very pretty.

SIZE AND SHAPE: Over all, it is a small-leafed ivy. Some of the leaves are so small (one quarter of an inch) that they could be classified as miniatures. Others are one to one and one half inches long. The leaves have five to seven lobes. Most have two pairs of lateral lobes very sharply defined, as fan-shaped ivies are, and a long terminal lobe, but their terminal lobes are extended, thus giving a resemblance to the Bird's Foot group.

COLOR: The younger leaves have a rich, grass-green color. The older ones are a jade-green.

HABIT OF GROWTH: 'Pixie' is a slow-growing, compact plant. On some vines the leaves are clustered. On others they are densely shingled.

CULTURE: 'Pixie' can take more sun than most ivies. I've grown mine in a very sunny window, and the color has not bleached out.

Hedera Helix 'Triton'

'Triton' is different from all other fan-shaped ivies because of its long, tapering, twisted lobes. Even the petioles are twisted or kinked and often the stems are slightly zig-zag. The leaves are elegant and beautiful and show off to their best advantage in a hanging basket.

It's not a great plant for outdoors because its sprawling habit makes it untidy as a ground cover and it doesn't fasten itself well to walls. It is a great collector's item.

SIZE AND SHAPE: 'Triton' generally has five lobes, but what makes it so interesting is that the 3 long, narrow, twisted central lobes may be cut nearly three-quarters of the way to the midrib. The main veins are conspicuously raised. The summer leaves may only have three lobes and the large middle lobe is not quite as twisted.

COLOR: Leaves are dark green.

HABIT OF GROWTH: In addition to its sprawling habit referred to above it also frequently sports ivy-ivy type leaves which should be pinched off.

CULTURE: Semi-shade.

The Curlies

CHAPTER EIGHT

PLEASE FORGIVE ME if I rhapsodize about curly ivies. I think they are beautiful in the way their leaves curl and overlap in delightful ripples, ruffles, and pleats. The leaf formations are so remarkably intricate, the texture so delightful to touch, and their shades of green so exquisite that to me they are the spellbinders of the ivy world.

As a group, the Curlies will take more sunshine than most ivies (except the Variegateds), but full sun tends to fade their color. Curlies need a refreshing dousing in the sink more often than most ivies because of all those ripples and ruffles in their leaves that provide a great haven for spider mites.

Hedera Helix 'Telecurl'

'Telecurl' is a beauty that originated in the 1950s. Because of its shape, I believe it to be a sport of 'Merion Beauty', which in turn is a sport of 'Pittsburgh', and therefore it is fairly hardy. 'Telecurl' looks beautiful in flower arrangements. When the arrangement loses life, make cuttings of 'Telecurl'.

SIZE AND SHAPE: Its leaves are so deeply curled that some look as though there were three leaves coming out of a single petiole. Each leaf is a ruffled beauty unto itself with no consistent method of curling.

The number of lobes vary. On the three-lobed leaves, the lobes are more or less of equal size, whereas those leaves with five lobes have larger terminal and lateral lobes, smaller basals. Occasionally you'll find a seven-lobed leaf. Leaves vary in size from one to one and one half inches.

With 'Telecurl', as with many ivies, there is a seasonal variation in the size, shape and compactness of the leaf as well as in the degree of branching. In summer when growth is more rapid the leaves of 'Telecurl' are larger and less curly and the lobes are shallower.

COLOR: The color in the younger leaves is a lovely apple-green. As the leaf grows older it becomes avocado-green. The veins are hardly discernible and are a bit paler than the leaf itself. Sinuses are deep.

HABIT OF GROWTH: It is a compact plant with a strong tendency to branch from its base. Since it's a slow grower, it will take some time filling in an area, but once it has, you'll have a rippling, wavy carpet of green.

CULTURE: You can grow this beauty outdoors south of New York, but be sure to place it where it will have some protection against winter's havoc.

Hedera Helix 'Manda Crested'

Exciting! Gorgeous! There aren't enough adjective to describe
my favorites of all the curly ivies. Mrs. Otto Beuttner of Stamford, Connecticut, an award-winning gardener whose garden

always has the most unusual plants, introduced me to this variety. She used it to edge a lovely winding path and also planted it in a fluffy mass in front of a perennial bed. She gave me a few cuttings several years ago. From just a handful of cuttings I was able to cover an entire area with this very handsome and productive ivy.

SIZE AND SHAPE: The three-inch leaves are five-lobed with a long terminal lobe and laterals almost at right angles to it. The basal lobes are about half the size of the laterals. In most cases all the lobes curve inward giving the leaf a smaller appearance than it really has. The overall effect is a crested, elegantly curled leaf.

COLOR: 'Manda Crested' has light green leaves with still lighter veins, which grow upright on a reddish petiole. The new growth is a soft pea-green and has a faint soft-rose line along the margins. Occasionally one can observe a warm haze of rose over the entire leaf.

HABIT OF GROWTH: This plant has closely spaced ruffles of leaves. 'Manda Crested' has a strong tendency to branch from the base of the plant and then tumble into waves of soft green foliage. Its leaves are usually uniform in size.

CULTURE: If given some protection from winter sun and drying winds it is hardy outdoors. It was propagated by W. A. Manda of New Jersey and is hardy like 'Merion Beauty' from which it sported.

Hedera Helix 'Fluffy Ruffles'

Its name describes this ivy perfectly. This plant is as deeply ruffled as 'Telecurl' but with a larger, more spectacular leaf. It is a truly magnificent plant. Try growing 'Fluffy Ruffles' in a planter to-gether with geraniums. The effect is worthwhile.

SIZE AND SHAPE: Five to seven shallow lobes on rounded leaves about two inches in diameter characterize 'Fluffy Ruffles'. Very undulating and crisply frilled, the lobes curl back to the petiole making each leaf a perfect ruffle. The sinuses are rather shallow.

COLOR: Darker green than 'Manda Crested', it's about the color of U.S. money. The young leaves have an unusually delicate shade of apple-green. The raised veins verge on yellow and are very prominent.

HABIT OF GROWTH: Its long graceful veins seem to tumble from the plant. Since it is very self-branching, the effect is a riot of fluffy ruffles.

CULTURE: This is another curly ivy you can grow outdoors if you are careful where you put it. Its softly textured leaves do not like winter sun.

Hedera Helix 'Curly Locks'

"Curly Locks" is a curly because of the way the edges are curled and crimped. Unlike 'Manda Crested', which has a leaf that ripples and undulates, 'Curly Locks' is more or less flat, but has so much curliness on the edge that the leaf seems fluted. As with other curly ivies, the degree of curliness varies with the growing conditions. The faster the growth, the less curly the ivy. Leaves grown in shade are larger and less curly than leaves from the same plant exposed to sun.

'Curly Locks' is often confused with 'Parsley Crested' which is very similar. To tell the difference you almost have to have them side by side. 'Parsley Crested' has smaller leaves and the leaf margin is more finely crimped.

SIZE AND SHAPE: The three to five-lobed leaves are minutely frilled. The curliness is expressed both as a strongly but un-evenly fluted margin (undulate up and down) and as a leaf blade that is somewhat folded or cupped upward with the lobes tips curled downward. The petiole is about as long as the midrib but looks shorter due to overlapping leaf bases.

COLOR: The older leaves are parsley-green while the younger ones are apple-green. The veins are quite pronounced, appearing white on the older leaves and yellowish in the younger.

HABIT OF GROWTH: It is a trailing ivy that is only self branching if pinched. Try 'Curly Locks' as a contrasting plant in a bed with other perennials and in large baskets and patio planters. It should also be tried as a ground cover; its attractive curly foliage is a welcome contrast to the traditional flat ivy ground covers.

CULTURE: Give it plenty of sun for really frilled leaves. Hardy to zone 4 if planted deeply. See page 21.

Hedera Helix 'Ivalace'

The wet shine of 'Ivalace' leaves is breathtaking. The plant is a great favorite for use in topiaries because of the highly polished look of the glossy leaves. It is the smallest of all the Curlies, but its curl is minimal.

I used 'Ivalace' quite successfully on a large-size topiary shaped like a flamingo, but I was a little unhappy with the number of large leaves the plant developed. Since I tend to be a perfectionist about shape and form with my topiaries, I spent too much time picking off all the leaves that were over one inch.

SIZE AND SHAPE: Five-lobed, slightly leathery leaves with an undulating edge describe 'Ivalace'. The leaves vary in size from one half inch to one and one half inches, with the average leaf about one inch from the point where the petiole joins the leaf to the tip of the terminal lobe. The terminal lobe is sharply pronounced as are the lateral and basal lobes. The leaf has deep sinuses, and the effect is almost the shape of a maple leaf.

COLOR: The older leaves are a dark, rich, shiny green. The young leaves have a lime-green color. Veins are quite pronounced on the older leaves and are the same lime-green as the new growth. 'Ivalace' is the glossiest of all the ivies.

HABIT OF GROWTH: A self-branching, many-leaved plant, it roots quite easily but is a slow grower.

CULTURE: Indoors, give it plenty of light and moisture but no soggy soil. Place it in the sink once a week and give it a good spray of water, particularly on the underside of the leaves, to discourage any spider mites that might be poised for the kill. Outdoors plant deep and give plenty of winter protection.

Hedera Helix 'California'

'California' is one of the best all-around, all purpose ivies for wreaths, baskets and larger topiaries. It is also useful for ground covers and wall covers in sun and shade. It is quite self-branching. It is the least curly of the ivies in this chapter. What I like best is the abundance of the leaves and the way they overlap each other.

SIZE AND SHAPE: 'California' is a five-lobed ivy that is medium sized with leaves that are about as broad as they are long. The veins are slightly raised. It is not the outside edge of the leaf that is curly as with other Curlies. 'California' curls near the base of the leaf where the petiole is attached and in the "valley" between the lobes. Like all curly ivies, the leaves are less curly in summer when growth is rapid.

COLOR: Girl Scout green.

HABIT OF GROWTH: The ease with which 'California sports and reverts can either be fun or annoying, depending on what type of gardener you are. One grower reported that he observed ivy that looked like 'Ivalace', 'Telecurl', 'Big Deal', 'California Fan', 'Pixie', and 'Cockle Shell' - all growing on 'California' stems!

CULTURE: OK in sun or shade.

The Heart Shapes

CHAPTER NINE

SOME IVY FANCIERS have nicknamed this ivy class, "the Valentines". Heart shaped they certainly are and very easy to identify. The varieties in this group are all very similar with true heart-shaped leaves, and they differ mainly in the size of their leaf.

In this group my favorites are 'Deltoidea' (also known as 'Sweetheart') because of the true heart shape of each leaf, and 'Garland' because of its profusion of leaves that densely clothe the stems.

One idiosyncrasy should be mentioned here. The majority of ivies growing outdoors when they reach their adult stage (when they stop climbing) tend to lose their sinuses and take on a heart shape. Don't be misled if you see a heart-shaped ivy growing outdoors and call it a Heart Shape when its juvenile plant is a member of an entirely different group.

Hedera Helix 'Deltoidea'

'Deltoidea', popularly called the Sweetheart ivy, because of its valentine-shaped leaves is popular with flower arrangers, not only for its obvious uses for romantic celebrations, but because its stems are stiff and lend themselves to arrangement without difficulty.

Normally, I don't like to use a leaf-shine spray. However the leaves on 'Deltoidea' are so perfectly heart shaped that you may want to show them off. Wash them spotlessly clean and then spray them with leaf shine.

SIZE AND SHAPE: Leaves are about one to one and one half inches long and wide and perfectly heart shaped. My 'Deltoidea' is quite old and in the considerable length of time I have had it, not one leaf has varied from its heart shape.

COLOR: Dark green leaves with pale green veins.

HABIT OF GROWTH: The stems are thick and stiffer than most ivies. It is not self-branching, but if you pinch it back regularly you will get a fuller plant.

CULTURE: It's a pleasure to give this one loving care although it doesn't require much attention. Partial sun, moist soil with good drainage, and a weekly dousing are all that it needs as a pot plant. Outdoors it is happiest climbing up a wall.

Hedera Helix 'Garland'

If this plant had been around in Bacchus's day, his followers would have selected it for the wreath on his head. The heart-shaped leaves truly do form a garland on their vine. On my Thanksgiving table, I have used 'Garland' coming out of a cornucopia accented with pomegranates and persimmons. Very decorative.

SIZE AND SHAPE: 'Garland' is a compact bushy plant that makes mounds of overlapping large heart shaped leaves that are about one and one half times as long as broad.

COLOR: Leaves are a bright green with lighter green, well-defined veins.

HABIT OF GROWTH: Bess Shippy who introduced 'Garland' in 1951 said that it has "... leaves that overlap until they look like wide platted garlands." It is a good ground cover for Zone 7 or warmer.

CULTURE: Find a spot in your home with northerly light. Outdoors plant deep and give winter protection.

Hedera Helix 'Teardrop'

It isn't hard to guess how 'Teardrop' got its name. It really looks like a tear drop. It was discovered in the United States in the 1950s.

SIZE AND SHAPE: A pretty little ivy with teardrop shaped leaves.

COLOR: Rich, shiny green foliage with light green veins.

HABIT OF GROWTH: Readily self-branching with trailing vines. Makes elegant mounds of foliage.

CULTURE: 'Teardrop' is an excellent small-leaved outdoor ivy. It is very hardy and established plants have shown no winter damage under trees when temperatures have gone to minus 15° F.

Hedera Colchica 'Sulphur Heart'

This heart-shaped ivy is not Hedera Helix, but Hedera Colchica. The Persian or Colchic ivy is native to the region south of the Caspian and westward through the Caucasus to Asiatic Turkey. Botanists talk about its scale-like hairs and the number of rays it has under the microscope. I talk about its striking, bold leaves with their wonderful splash of gold in the center. These colorful big leaves grow so fast they can quickly cover a tree trunk in a few years. And like H. helix 'Gold Heart', H. colchica 'Sulphur Heart' doesn't lose its gold center.

SIZE AND SHAPE: The leaves are large and one to one and one half times as long as wide so the shape of the heart is elongated.

COLOR: Leaves are light green with irregular splashes of gold. The veins are slightly lighter green except where they traverse the variegated patch, where they are yellow.

HABIT OF GROWTH: This one, like all the Colchic ivies, is a dramatic large-scale climber. Because it is such a vigorous grower it is a fine plant for walls, fences and as a ground cover.

CULTURE: At Longwood Gardens in their hardiness trials along a west-facing wall 'Sulphur Heart' grew vigorously in full sun.

Hedera Colchica 'Dentata'

British plantsman/author Ronald Whitehouse writes that the unlobed matt leaves of Hedera colchica 'Dentata' "... are often up to nine inches long, so it is not surprising to find that it is sometimes called 'Elephant Ears'." And Peter Q. Rose says that it is hardy in Britain and most of Europe and as far north as Zone 5 in the USA. I give you this information from these experts because I have not grown 'Dentata' personally, although I must say that from their descriptions I *should* be growing it.

You can always tell that a colchica is not a helix by crushing a leaf. If it smells like celery it is colchica. The fragrance appears to be water soluble because when the stems are immersed in water, the water become aromatic.

SIZE AND SHAPE: Very large and about as broad as it is long. Irregular heart shape.

COLOR: Rich pea-green, veins light green.

HABIT OF GROWTH: Unusually vigorous and strongly vining. Also makes an excellent ground cover for large areas.

CULTURE: My friends report that it will take full sun. Just give it plenty of space because it grows so quickly.

The Variegateds

CHAPTER TEN

THE COLORS of the Variegateds run from white to yellow~ splashed on the ivy green. They certainly add a bright note as potted plants and in arrangements.

Ivies can be variegated in many different ways, and unless you study them carefully one Variegated seems much like another. But as you study them you'll find that some leaves are more variegated along the edges while others will be variegated white or yellow over most of the leaf. Still others will have not only lovely white and yellow patches in distinct areas but also patches of two shades of green.

Then too, as in the case of 'Tricolor', some Variegateds if grown outdoors will change color during the autumn and winter. Because the light-colored sections produce little or no chlorophyll those ivies with more green in them than variegation will root more easily than those with a larger amount of white or yellow.

A curious habit of the Variegateds (and sometimes very annoying) is their tendency to abandon their variegated pattern and become all-green leaves. I have found that the growth of the colored foliage is stimulated when insufficiently fed. I always root my variegateds in tiny two-inch pots so that when I need them in a flower arrangement I can tuck the little pots into a vase along with my flowers without having to cut my ivy.

Hedera Helix 'Gold Heart'

'Gold Heart' has a sunny splash of yellow on a green leaf, courtesy of Italy from which it came. It is my favorite of all the Variegateds.

SIZE AND SHAPE: This is a relatively small-leafed ivy but cannot be classed as miniature. The leaves have three to five lobes and vary from one half inch to two inches. The lobes are sharply pointed.

COLOR: Here's where 'Gold Heart' is outstanding. The green on the edge is a darkly rich green. In the center there is a dollop of a rich gold-yellow. The plant looks as if the sun touched it and wouldn't go away. The yellow in 'Gold Heart' is the strongest yellow found in any of the Variegateds. The stems and petioles are reddish.

HABIT OF GROWTH: 'Gold Heart' readily sports half-green, half-variegated stems and, frequently all green stems. The more vigorous all-green shoots must be pruned out in order to avoid the plant being overtaken by green stems.

Although 'Gold Heart' has widely spaced leaves, it can be used in open frame topiary, where it can be tied to an outline frame, such as a heart-shaped topiary. It makes a beautiful wall or trellis cover outside but reversions need to be pruned out.

CULTURE: Indoors grow 'Gold Heart' in a sunny window to prevent its losing its color. Outdoors it does best in three quarter sun. It roots slowly, but once well-rooted it's a tough survivor.

Hedera Helix 'Gold Dust'

Take a green leaf, sprinkle it with gold dust until it has a rich, mottled, look and you'll have the appearance of 'Gold Dust'. I first discovered 'Gold Dust' one spring on the top of a man-made waterfall just as dusk was falling. Surrounded by the spring green of the shrubs and trees, it looked like a huge pot of gold. It was growing in a hugh flat bowl set on a rock, with the plant's graceful branches tumbling over the edges as if trying to reach the waterfall below it.

SIZE AND SHAPE: The leaf size of 'Gold Dust' is more variable than most ivies. Averagely the leaf is about one and one-half to two inches in length and breadth, however sometimes an entire stem can have enormous leaves at least twice the size. This usually happens in the spring. As growth continues, the leaf sizes will become more normal sized and abnormal growth less obvious. Frequently leaves may grow so fast that they are distorted in size and shape.

COLOR: The Variegateds can be broadly broken down into two groups; those with an overall color pattern and those with distinct areas of color separation 'Gold Dust' is in the first category with its flecks of unripened-lemon yellow and rich dark green, which often merge into a very pleasant blotched or mottled effect. The older leaves tend to lose this mottled effect although a hint of it usually remains.

HABIT OF GROWTH: 'Gold Dust' is a slow grower and not readily self-branching. Cut it back and force it to branch. Root the cuttings.

Hedera Helix 'Glacier'

Whenever I contemplate the Variegateds I become awed by nature's artwork. A casual glance at 'Glacier' tells you it has cream and green colors, but study it, particularly the young leaves, and you'll see what a magnificent technician nature really is. Its color and the arrangement of the color on the leaves is beautiful.

It is often difficult to distinguish the various Variegateds from each other, even when you place them side by side. Nature puts an individual touch on each one of them, sometimes so subtle you have to hunt for it. Try a half-dozen plants of 'Glacier' indoors for winter brightness. Use it as a contrasting color in your hanging baskets.

SIZE AND SHAPE: 'Glacier's' leaves are five-lobed and small. They measure from one half inch to one and one half inches and are roughly triangular. Because of the angle of the terminal lobe, the basal lobes don't appear to be very developed. The veins are raised, and the leaves are somewhat leathery to the touch.

COLOR: 'Glacier's' leaves run from light gray-green to dark gray-green and are outlined with creamy white edges. Occasionally you'll find a leaf more creamy than green. Sometimes, and particularly on the new shoots, you'll find an edge of pink. The veins are cream colored.

HABIT OF GROWTH: A reluctant rooter and a slow grower makes 'Glacier' ideal for spots where you do not want the ivy to take over. It has good vining growth. If you want to force branching, do a little pruning.

CULTURE: Use a well-drained soil and don't ever let it get water-logged. Be patient when making cuttings. Just when you think they'll never root, the roots appear. 'Glacier' can be grown outdoors all year round in areas south of New Jersey. North of New Jersey be sure to plant deeply and give winter protection.

Hedera Helix
'*Sagittaefolia Variegata*'

This delightful beauty is a variegated Bird's Foot. It has all the good color of the Variegateds as well as the delicately shaped form of the Bird's Foot ivies. In Europe it is called Koniger's Variegated.

SIZE AND SHAPE: 'Sagittaefolia' is a Bird's Foot leaf, but it looks as if the bird had flat feet. Since each leaf is very flat and grows in the same direction from its petiole, the entire vine takes on a "just ironed" look.

The leaves are generally an inch long, but because the terminal lobe is so long and slender, they appear to be smaller than they really are.

COLOR: Strongly variegated. Generally creamy white around the edges with two shades of gray-green in the center. Occasionally the gray-green has a speckled look. The green of the new growth is almost apple green. The veins are whitish and look particularly pretty when seen against the gray-green.

HABIT OF GROWTH: The vines are heavily leafed. If you cut them back, the new growth will shoot out a profusion of leaves causing the vine to be ladened with a layered cluster of leaves. Really beautiful.

CULTURE: Keep in a west window. It likes a little sun.

Hedera Helix 'Buttercup'

This is the yellowest of all ivies, but only when grown in full sun is it the real buttercup color.

SIZE AND SHAPE: Take the color away and the shape is very close to Baltic, English, or 'Pittsburgh'. All lobes are sharply pronounced. The length of the terminal lobe is almost the same as the width of the lateral lobes. The leaves are from three-quarters to two inches.

COLOR: In the 1974 edition of this book I said the nursery from which I obtained 'Buttercup' described it as "freely suffused bright gold yellow" but that *never* - not in sun or shade - had my leaves become a bright golden yellow. Since then I have seen lots of "bright golden yellow" 'Buttercup' ivies. The problem I have is that I live in the woods and what I call full sun in a woodland condition is not really full sun!

HABIT OF GROWTH: It is a vigorous grower but is inclined to get long and straggly. Cut it back severely to make it a more compact plant. It is not self-branching. 'Buttercup' is a climbing ivy and not recommended for ground cover where it will lose its unique golden coloring.

CULTURE: Grow it in full, full sun.

Hedera Helix 'Gold Child'

'Gold Child' wasn't around when I wrote the 1974 edition of this book. Now it is so readily available it is frequently found in the supermarket. 'Gold Child' is lovely as a pot plant and in baskets, but is not reliably hardy. Unless you live in a mild climate, treat it as a half-hardy perennial.

SIZE AND SHAPE: The medium to large leaves are shaped like the Ivy-Ivies with five broad, slightly rounded lobes. The leaves are basically "flat". The leaf stalks are long, typically one to one and one-half times the length of the leaf.

COLOR: 'Gold Child' appears to be one of those variegated ivies whose coloring is strongly dependent on the environment in which it is grown. Greenhouse-grown specimens are green with a unique, distinctive, bright green-gold edge, but when the same plant is grown out of doors, the marginal variegation takes on a creamy white color, and the center becomes a mixture of various shades of gray. With cooler weather in the fall the creamy white leaves become tinged with pink, so that the leaves are a beautiful mixture of pink, cream, chartreuse, greens and grays. Dr. Sabina Sulgrove, The American Ivy Society Registrar, reports that leaves of 'Gold Child' that were formed during the Ohio summer 1988 heat wave (with temperatures over 100' F.) were cream-colored (and small because of the drought) but as soon as the temperatures dropped and the rains came, the newly formed làrger leaves were green centered with a chartreuse margin.

HABIT OF GROWTH: Although the stems are not noticeably self-branching, the leaves are large enough to nicely clothe the stems. Pinch it back to make a fuller plant.

CULTURE: Peter Q. Rose reports that 'Gold Child' is intolerant of under or over-watering. Outdoors plant deeply and give winter protection. See page 21.

Hedera Helix 'Schaefer Three'

'Schaefer Three' is one of the most popular variegated foliage plants in the trade today, both here in the United States and in Europe. It is popular, not because of the shape of the leaves which are Ivy-Ivy shaped, but because of the unusual variegation of the leaves. Generally they have a green border followed by an irregular band of white. In the center is a splash of various shades of gray-green. I say "generally" because the plant is so variable. In the course of a year the same stem can have leaves with white centers and green blotches that, closer to the margins, fuse together to make an irregular green border. Still others will have leaves with more green that white looking like a more green-colored 'Calico'. And again on the same stem all the leaves are green.

SIZE AND SHAPE: Medium-sized Ivy-Ivy shaped leaves.

COLOR: Green, white, gray-green (See first paragraph).

HABIT OF GROWTH: It is not self-branching so pinch it back to help it make more shoots.

CULTURE: My friend has grown it outdoors in 20' F below zero.

Hedera Helix 'Fantasia'

There is a lot of discussion in the ivy world about 'Fantasia' and whether or not it is a sport of 'Pittsburgh Variegated'. The speckling is a little different, but it is close enough to cause the controversy. And you all know how plant experts love controversy! Wherever it came from, it is a beautiful variegated ivy. The new leaves are white to creamy-white with evenly scattered green speckles and blotches. As the leaves mature, they become a medium green with faint speckles.

SIZE AND SHAPE: Leaves are about one and one-half inches - a little longer than broad with five lobes. Shaped like an Ivy-Ivy.

COLOR: 'Fantasia' can be differentiated from other white and green speckled ivies by the conspicuous white speckled veins that are still visible when the leaf starts to turn green. And it is one of the many variegated ivies whose variegated coloring appears to be seasonal. In the summer (heat) leaves may become nearly all green, although usually some leaves can be found with white speckles.

HABIT OF GROWTH: It is not self-branching and unless pruned regularly the long vines can seem stringy. Pruning it will produce a bushier plant with nice new white speckled variegations.

CULTURE: If you live in a cold climate it may die in the winter. Notwithstanding, ivy grower Gillia Hawke, who lives in Ohio, reported that her 'Fantasia' has made it through the winter.

Hedera Helix 'Calico'

'Calico' is a gorgeous green and white variegated five-lobed curly ivy with bright green splotches scattered all over the leaf. Really outstanding. It looks like another popular European ivy called 'Stift Neuburg' which is available in the United States at nurseries specializing in ivy. The American Ivy Society registrar, Dr. Sabina Sulgrove, says the way to tell the difference tween the two plants is to notice that 'Stift Neuburg' has a dark green edging and a predominantly white center with dark green flecks. Unless I have the two plants in my hand I find it difficult to tell the difference.

'Calico' also looks like 'Kolibri', another variegated curly. The way to tell the difference between them according to Dr. Donald G. Huttleston, Plant Taxonomist at Longwood Gardens, is that 'Calico' has the white scattered and not concentrated toward the margin, and that 'Kolibri' has more gray-green splotches. An interesting display at a flower show would be to put the three of them side by side and ask the experts to guess which is which. Don't invite me to come - I might guess wrong!

SIZE AND SHAPE: Leaves are one and one-quarter to one and three-quarters inches long and wide.

COLOR: Rich green and white.

HABIT OF GROWTH: There is a profusion of leaves and because the plant is so readily self-branching the total effect is spectacular.

CULTURE: It is cold sensitive so be careful where you plant it. I lost most of my 'Calico' where I live in Woodstock, New York, even though I covered it in the winter. Maybe I didn't plant it deeply enough.

Hedara Canariensis '*Gloire de Marengo*'

If you want a very fast growing ivy with large glossy leaves that are strongly variegated, 'Gloire de Marengo' is a great choice. The leaves are green or gray-green in the center and creamy-white on the edge.

When I was a little girl in California 'Gloire de Marengo' grew so vigorously in my mother's garden that it had a trunk - literally a trunk - as big around as my forearm. The California Highway Department also grows it as a ground cover alongside the freeways where grass maintenance is difficult.

But please note I am talking about California. Where I now live in Woodstock, New York, I can't grow it except as a pot plant. But is truly lovely in a basket or as a trained pyramid. Many offices use it for interior landscaping.

SIZE AND SHAPE: The leaves are large, three to four inches long, but may be smaller under poorer conditions.

COLOR: The center of the leaf is splashed with different shades of green and gray-green which intrude into the wide, creamy-white edge of the leaf. Stems are wine red.

HABIT OF GROWTH: It needs plenty of space in the garden it is very robust and fast to grow. It is a vining ivy, good for climbing, for ground cover or for garden walls.

CULTURE: In California even a bad gardener couldn't kill it. In areas where there are hard frosts even a good gardener can't grow it. In Britain Peter Q. Rose reports that it "... survives very severe winters but with much loss of leaf."

$\mathcal{M}iniatures$

CHAPTER ELEVEN

MOST OF the ivies in this group are true miniatures. That is, they are plants shaped in every way like larger-leafed ivy except that the leaves are considerably smaller, less than one inch in length.

Miniatures are ideal plants for people living in small apartments. There is not only much joy in growing them, but they also take up so little space that they can even be grouped under a glass bell or a lucite cake dome like a miniature greenhouse.

Miniatures can give a spectacular effect in stuffed topiaries, provided, however that you have lots and lots of patience or lots and lots of cuttings because they are slow growers.

Hedera Helix 'Jubilee'

This miniature is one of my favorites, and it's quite likely to be yours too. It's got everything. Tiny. Colorful. Compact growth. It's even self-branching. Each little snub-nosed leaf (of which there is a profusion) is a sparkling beauty. 'Jubilee' is a must in your collection.

SIZE AND SHAPE: The smallest leaves are no more than one-half inch long and wide. The largest leaves are no more than three quarter inch long and one-half inch wide. The leaves are irregularly shaped, but most have three to five lobes.

It is almost impossible to describe the leaf shape because there are so many different shapes on each vine. On some, the terminal lobe is long with no hint of sinuses, which makes the leaf look like a teardrop. On others, the lateral lobes are clearly defined, and those leaves look like Ivy-Ivies. Then, there are other that have a large lateral lobe on one side only, and some have to lateral lobes that are differently shaped. Despite this marvelous variety, 'Jubilee' is an easy ivy to identify because of its very tiny leaves and variegation.

COLOR: Its three colors vie with its shape for beauty. The light silvery-green leaves are edged creamy-white with dollops of dark-green splashed on the leaves. No two leaves are colored the same. Even the veins are capricious. On some, they are hardly noticeable. On others they are raised and whitish.

HABIT OF GROWTH: 'Jubilee' is a slow, slow grower but is freely self-branching with a profusion of leaves on every vine. The leaves grow from the base of the plant, giving it a very bushy look even in a young plant.

CULTURE: It's a sturdy plant that does not need to be pampered, but because it is so pretty and such a joy to handle, I find myself following ivy-culture rules to the letter and treating 'Jubilee' like a fragile baby, which it is not. Give it plenty of humidity, not too much food, some sun, or at least good strong light.

Hedera Helix 'Spetchley'

'Spectchley' is the ivy with the tiniest leaves. Smaller than your fingernail. It is an interesting little ivy that looks great planted in small rock crevices or along a border. It can also be used as a bonsai. For me its main drawback is that the stems are stiff and don't have ivy's usual graceful appearance.

'Spetchley' was discovered in 1962 growing in Spetchley Park in England. It wasn't really known in the United States until the middle 70's.

SIZE AND SHAPE: The leaves are less than one-half inch. Its leaves have three lobes with a prominent rounded terminal lobe and light diffuse veins.

COLOR: Dark green leaves which are leathery in texture. Perhaps because of the extremely small size of the leaf the texture seems thicker than it is.

HABIT OF GROWTH: Readily self-branching. It will creep or climb in rock gardens.

CULTURE: Hardy to Zone 4 if you plant deeply and give winter protection. See page 21.

Hedera Helix 'Midget'

'Midget' is a miniature version of 'Needlepoint', but if you want to be nomenclaturally correct don't call it 'Miniature Needlepoint'. It is not known if the 'Midget' which we grow in the United States is the same as 'Tres Coupe' grown in Europe. Peter Q. Rose, in his book "Ivies" tells the story of 'Tres Coupe' which gives me a giggle. He says that "... a keen British amateur gardener saw the plant in the garden of Roger de Vilmorin of the well-known French nursery firm. Accepting the generously offered plant he enquired the name: *'Je ne sais pas'*, replied his host, *'Il est tres coupe'*." 'Tres Coupe' it became.

The American 'Midget' came from Florida and the American Ivy Society research center received it in 1977.

SIZE AND SHAPE: Leaves are one-half to one inch and, like 'Needlepoint' are a Bird's Foot.

COLOR: Bright green.

HABIT OF GROWTH: It has a cascade of trails. The stems are densely covered with leaves.

CULTURE: Half sun. Hardy to Zone 4 if you plant deeply and give winter protection.

Hedera Helix 'Duck Foot'

'Duck Foot' is well named. It has masses on tiny mid-green leaves in the shape of a duck's foot. I have had great success with it in my garden in Woodstock, New York. Several years ago we had a terrible winter in New York when the weather turned cold, bitterly cold, very early in the season before the ground had any snow. Below 0' F. I had just put in a new ivy experimental garden with 100 plants each of 100 different cultivars. The plants had not been in the ground for more than 3 months when this unusual weather hit us which was just bad luck. Sad to say, I lost most of my new plants. Astonishing, however, was the fact that little 'Duck Foot' came through this harsh spell just fine and has now become a handsome ground cover.

SIZE AND SHAPE: Leaves are under one inch and the lobes are variable, but mainly rounded. Internodes and petioles are shot.

COLOR: Medium green.

HABIT OF GROWTH: 'Duck Foot' is self-branching with a profusion of leaves on its vines. It works very well in stuffed topiaries or wreaths.

CULTURE: I grow it in three-quarter sun.

Hedera Helix 'Lady Frances'

'Lady Frances' is a miniature that is also a Variegated and a Bird's Foot. It looks particularly beautiful in a hanging basket because when the long vines hang down the lateral branches turn upward. It is a highly desirable cultivar for all kinds of topiary where a fine-textured, gray-white contrast is required.

'Lady Frances' is a relatively new ivy and was submitted for registration with The American Ivy Society in 1991 by Mo Halawi, Director of Operations and Landscape Design at Weidner's Gardens in San Diego. He named it for Frances Rynearson who helped host the American Ivy Society Topiary Conference at the San Diego Zoo.

SIZE AND SHAPE: Leaves are small, highly asymmetrical about one inch or less and about as wide as long, although they often appear longer because of the elongated terminal lobe on the three-lobed leaves. But every lobe, and every leaf is different, both in shape and in coloration.

COLOR: This is a gray and white ivy. The central gray areas are splashed haphazardly with various shades of gray, sometimes overlaid with a deeper gray-green. The white border is also irregular, wider in some areas than others.

HABIT OF GROWTH: Strongly self-branching. The long vines produce bushy mats of foliage.

CULTURE: Half sun.

Hedera Helix 'Green Feather'

'Green Feather' is a miniature Bird's Foot ivy with three deeply cut, long narrow lobes. It has sometimes been known as 'Meagheri'. There is much controversy about its name which I want to tell you about because it explains why there is often controversy about ivy names. The rules of nomenclature state that the first name to be *published* is the name that has validity. 'Green Feather' is a sport discovered in 1939 by a Mr. Meagher, a nursery employee, in Albany, New York. In 1940 Bates, writing in the National Horticultural Magazine described the plant under the name 'Green Feather'. This was an authentic publication and therefore *that* became the valid name.

SIZE AND SHAPE: Leaves are about one inch with a very long, tapering terminal lobe. The lobes are cupped upward and folded along the midrib.

COLOR: Dark green, veins lighter green.

HABIT OF GROWTH: Trailing vines that are not really self-branching, but if you will regularly pinch it back it will become a much fuller plant. Looks beautiful in a hanging basket. Works well in a tabletop stuffed topiary.

CULTURE: Hardy to Zone 4. Plant deeply and give winter protection for at least three years.

Hedera Helix 'Little Diamond'

'Little Diamond' is a variegated miniature that really looks like its name. Most of the leaves are diamond shaped although it sometimes throws shoots that resemble 'Glacier'. It is an outstanding small shrubby ivy.

SIZE AND SHAPE: About one inch diamond-shaped leaves.

COLOR: Leaves are a gray-green with a white edge.

HABIT OF GROWTH: This self-branching ivy is a slow grower. You don't have to worry about it invading other plants. Best grown in a basket or in a rock garden.

CULTURE: Hardy to Zone 4. Plant deeply and give winter protection for at least three years. See page 21.

The Ivy-Ivies

CHAPTER TWELVE

THE OTHER chapters have dealt with ivies that are Curlies, Heart Shapes, Fans, Bird's Feet, Variegateds; and for the most part these are fairly easy to identify because they are unusual.

The plants in the group I call the Ivy-Ivies are the hardest of all to distinguish from each other because they are so similar-they look like everyone's idea of what ivy should look like. Almost all of them have pronounced terminal, basal, and lateral lobes. All have indented sinuses, and all resemble the *Hedera helix* or so-called English Ivy that most Americans think of when they think of ivy. The English, however, don't call *Hedera helix* "English". They call it "common" ivy.

Most of the ivies in this group will ivy outdoors in states south of New Jersey when planted in a protected spot out of the strong clear winter sun. A good rule to remember is that the ivies you plant outdoors will more likely be hurt by winter sun than by cold frosty air.

Hedera Helix 'Walthamensis'

'Walthamensis' is a small version of English Ivy. In fact, some people call it "Baby English". In the 1990's it became popular for use in nosegays and bouquets where a trailing vine is required.

SIZE AND SHAPE: An easy way to identify this plant is to look for the sharply indented sinuses on all five lobes. Often the basal lobes on ivy leaves are so small that to find them you have to examine a leaf minutely. But on 'Walthamensis' the basal lobes are clearly defined because of the depth of the sinuses. Leaves are from three-quarter inch to one and one-half inches long and wide.

COLOR: The new growth is a very lively shade of grass-green and tends to darken as it matures. Veins whitish.

HABIT OF GROWTH: 'Walthamensis' is a vining plant with no self-branching habit. Its vines are slender and flexible. It is a good climber.

CULTURE: This is a good plant for outdoor growth in places where there are narrow areas to cover because it does not "take over" as many ivies do. Needs good drainage. Hardy to Zone 4.

Hedera Helix 'Cascade'

'Cascade' does just that. It cascades with long self-branching stems. It differs from other ivy-ivies in that it has a curl in each sinus giving the leaves a slightly curly appearance.

SIZE AND SHAPE: About one and one-half inch in length and breadth. The new growth from the cascading stems is not up-right, but rather flattened into the same plane as the stem.

COLOR: Mid-green. Veins much lighter.

HABIT OF GROWTH: Because of its tendency to throw long, branching trails it is excellent in hanging baskets, wreaths and topiary.

CULTURE: Hardy to Zone 4 if you plant deeply and give winter protection.

Hedera Helix 'Thorndale'

If you live in an area that has really cold winters where the
temperature drops down to 25' F. below zero, this is the ivy for
you. 'Thorndale' looks like a typical "English Ivy" (which is

actually 'Hibernica') but its hardiness and disease resistance is quite different.

'Thorndale' was introduced in the late 1940's by Thorndale Farm nursery. This is the way their 1953 catalog describes it:

> "The mother plant (of 'Thorndale') has never once been hurts by temperatures even lower than 20' below zero nor by sleet, ice and severe weather changes when even such hardy deciduous vines as Boston Ivies froze to the ground.

> Several generations of this unusual hardy strain of ivy have been tested against other English types of ivy under varying growing conditions and even were planted in the most unfavorable situations. Thorndale ivy prospered when all others failed, including Baltic ivy."

SIZE AND SHAPE: Leaves are from two to three inches and are a little wider than long.

COLOR: Dark green with crisp white veins that are especially conspicuous in winter.

HABIT OF GROWTH: Not self-branching.

CULTURE: This one is a "toughie". It will take a lot of abuse and come through happily.

Hedera Helix 'Baltica'

'Baltica' is sometimes confused with 'Thorndale', but 'Baltica' is readily distinguished by its heart shaped leaves most of which have three rounded lobes.

'Baltica' is perhaps the oldest ground cover in the United States. Perhaps only 'Hibernica', the ivy commonly sold as plain English ivy, is older.

SIZE AND SHAPE: Leaves are medium-size, about one to one and one-quarter times as long as wide and are basically three-lobed with the majority of the leaves showing only three lobes.

COLOR: Rich green becoming darker as they mature. Very pronounced white veins in winter.

HABIT OF GROWTH: Not self-branching. Strong climber. When growing up a tree or any vertical surface, 'Baltica's' leaves are still three-lobed, but are more elongated and sharper lobed (an effect of shade).

CULTURE: Hardy to Zone 4.

Hedera Helix 'Hibernica'

When the first settlers came from Britain to America they are said to have brought 'Hibernica' with them, according to Margaret Beach, The American Ivy Society Historian. They wanted a reminder of their homeland.

In the trade 'Hibernica' is usually sold as "English Ivy" although it is really "Irish Ivy". I am told it is probably the most widely planted of all ivies. According to Peter Q. Rose in Britain there can be few churchyards, parks or stately homes where the unmistakable large, slightly upward folder, dull-green leaves of 'Hibernica' do not provide cover or background.

SIZE AND SHAPE: Very large thick leaves from three to five inches that are wider than long with a broad terminal lobe.

COLOR: Medium dull green with light gray-green veins.

HABIT OF GROWTH: Strongly vining and very vigorous. On walls or as a ground cover it benefits from an annual clipping.

CULTURE: Hardy to Zone 5.

Hedera Helix 'Pittsburgh'

'Pittsburgh' deserves its place in history because it is the first of the self-branching ivies. It was found by Paul S. Randolph of Verona, Pennsylvania in 1920. There is also a 'Pittsburgh Variegated'.

There are now a myriad of sports from 'Pittsburgh'. Even some variegated sports. One called 'Serenade' was discovered in 1978 by Brother Ingobert Heick at the Neuburg Monastery Nursery, Heidelberg, West Germany. It is quite lovely with a gold-blotched center.

SIZE AND SHAPE: This is a small-leaved ivy from one to two inches and about as long as broad with five lobes. The terminal and lateral lobes are pointed, while the basal lobes are rounded.

COLOR: Medium green with lighter veins.

HABIT OF GROWTH: Self-branching. It branches from every node on the stem make a very nice bushy plant. It climbs. It vines.

CULTURE: I have grown mine happily in Zone 5 for years.

The Oddities

CHAPTER THIRTEEN

THE IVIES I have categorized as "Oddities' are in that group because they simply do not fit into any other category. They do not look like ivy, and a novice would have difficult identifying them as ivy. They are unusually showy and decorative, but difficult to find. Each one is in a class by itself and has no similarity to any other generic group.

Hedera Helix 'Small Deal'

This is an oddball ivy. It doesn't seem to belong to the ivy family - the spinach family, yes. The leaves have a distinctly puckered appearance. Years ago when I got my first plant I isolated it from the rest of my ivies and sprayed it every three days with Malathion. It wasn't until a month had gone by - when the new shoots appeared and they were distorted in the same way as the older ones - that I realized this was 'Small Deal's' normal appearance.

SIZE AND SHAPE: Leaves are from one to two inches and about as long as broad. They twist and cup or fold upward. The leaf seems to be scalloped rather than having lobes and if it weren't so puckered it could be classified as a Fan shape.

COLOR: Dark green with thick veins.

HABIT OF GROWTH: The stems, although not self-branching, are nicely clothed with leaves. The stems are stout and stiff so that new growth on cuttings is upright for at least the first twelve inches or so until the stems are heavy enough to hang. Its stiff, somewhat erect growth pattern makes 'Small Deal' an excellent candidate as an accent plant in protected rock gardens. 'Small Deal' would also be good for miniaturizing as a bonsai plant. It is too big, however, to be used for instant bonsai, in which a plant can be transferred to a bonsai pot (without top pruning or wiring) and assume the shape of an aged bonsai plant.

CULTURE: Hardy to Zone 5.

Hedera Helix 'Congesta'

The way 'Congesta's' leaves grow they remind you of a ladder - one leaf right on top of another. It looks great in a rock garden growing alongside 'Conglomerata'. 'Congesta' stands erect. 'Conglomerata' creeps. Both have the same dark leathery look.

SIZE AND SHAPE: Leaves are small and have almost no lobes.

HABIT OF GROWTH: The leaves are arranged in two opposite rows directly above each other. Not self-branching.

COLOR: Dark green, veins light green.

CULTURE: Hardy to Zone 7. I had success for a couple of years in Woodstock, New York (Zone 5), but when a really cold winter hit us, I lost my 'Congesta'. See page 21.

Hedera Helix 'Conglomerata'

This is a most decorative ivy and reminiscent of a bonsai form. It does not have the familiar grace and flow of most ivies, but it has an exquisite style all its own. It would be right at home in a garden in Japan or in any formal setting. It can be used with dramatic effect in a dish garden on your coffee table.

'Conglomerata' is a close relative of *Hedera helix* 'Erecta', and like this plant, it has a stiff habit of growth. Don't let its modern look fool you. It is not a new sport. The *London Gardener's Chronicle*, back in June 1871, referred to it as the "new Ivy" shown by the Royal Horticultural Society.

SIZE AND SHAPE: The branches are stiff and mostly erect. The effect is completely modern. The three- to five-lobed leaves, crinkly and curled, cluster together so tightly that the look is almost contorted. The lateral lobe is often missing. There terminal lobe is rounded and the sinuses wide. Its stems grow upward like candles on a Christmas tree.

COLOR: 'Conglomerata' is a dark, dull green and quite beautiful in its matted sheen. The veins are very pronounced and gray.

HABIT OF GROWTH: Dwarf in form, the plant does not climb but rather strikes a pose. I have one that resembles an oriental dancer. For a striking effect,silhouette it against a white rock in your garden.

CULTURE: If you're going to grow it indoors, put it where it will receive plenty of light and don't forget to give it a weekly dousing. It's tougher than it looks and can be planted outdoors to Zone 6.

Hedera Helix 'Erecta'

This unique ivy is similar to 'Conglomerata' and one of the best rock garden specimens I know. It really does credit to its name and one you've seen it you'll never forget it. The problem with it is that it is hard to purchase because so few people have it. As its name implies, it grows upwardly erect, very reminiscent of a desert cactus.

'Erecta' can be trained to grow in the form you want if you guide it when it's young with a copper or galvanized wire. The stems, as they grow older, will grow thick, and when the wire is cut away the plant will stay in the shape to which it has been trained.

SIZE AND SHAPE: It is the shape of strength. The stout twigs and stems have very pointed leaves that are shaped like a triangle and rigidly arranged opposite each other. They remind me of the paper cut-out ladders children used to make. The three- to five-lobed leaves are very thick and leathery. The terminal lobe is long. The basal lobes are not strongly defined.

COLOR: 'Erecta' is a rich gray-green with pronounced gray veins.

HABIT OF GROWTH: 'Erecta' can rightly be called the maverick of the ivy family. its branches grow upward as if in defiance of all its relatives. It is a very slow grower, but if you have the heart to cut a stem, it would give a strong accent in a "line" flower arrangement. However, before you cut a stem remember that it will take your plant considerable time to grow another stem as long.

The largest plant I've seen is two feet tall. Mine is about one and one half feet and is the senior ivy citizen of my plant room.

CULTURE: As long as it is not exposed to the drying wind of winter, it can be grown outdoors all year round to Zone 6.

Starter's Collection

Miniature
  'Midget'

Bird's Foot
  'Irish Lace'

Fans
  'California Fan'

Curlies
  'Manda Crested'

Variegateds
  'Gold Heart'
  'Calico'

Heart Shape
  'Garland'

Oddities
  'Conglomerata'

Ivy-Ivies
  'Walthamensis'

Nay, Nay!   Not Ivy

"Ivy" That Isn't Ivy

THERE ARE many plants that are called "ivy" but are not. These "ivies" include, among others:

- Grape Ivy   *Cissus rhombifolia*

- Devil's Ivy or Pothos   *Scindapsus aureus*

- German or Parlor Ivy   *Senecio mikanioides*

- Kenilworth Ivy   *Cymbalaria muralis*

- Kangaroo Ivy   *Cissus antarctica*

- Boston or Japanese Ivy   *Parthenocissus tricuspidata*

- Poison Ivy   *Rhus radicans*

Most of these make very good house plants (with the exception of Poison Ivy), but they are not members of the *Hedera* family or even remotely related. Some are very similar in appearance to real ivy, and for that reason they are included in this book so that you won't confuse them with the real thing.

Grape Ivy

This plant has bright olive-green foliage with bronze tones. The shiny three-part leaves are shaped like the leaves on Poison Ivy and are light to dark olive green with the bronze tint on the new growth. The underside of the leaves, as well as the younger stems, are covered with a fuzz of tiny, soft brown hairs. Its soil must be kept moist but not soaked. Grape Ivy is a native of South America.

Devil's Ivy or Pothos

This plant if often confused with Philodendron because the leaf shape is very similar. A native of the South Pacific Islands, it has heart-shaped leaves from two to four inches in length. Some leaves are marbled with pure white, while others show streaks of cream or yellow. Some are pure green. If kept in a dark location their coloring will become somewhat subdued with some leaves becoming completely green. Devil's Ivy is practically indestructible, but given adequate light and the privilege of drying out between waterings, it will respond with a colorful growth that most house plants cannot surpass.

German or Parlor Ivy

A native of South Africa, believe it or not, German Ivy is sometimes mistaken for *Hedera* because its leaves are similar in shape, but their color is a brighter green. The coarsely toothed leaves grow on a viny stem and trails or climbs. Mature plants form clusters of small, bright yellow flowers. They grow very fast and must be tip-pruned regularly for a compact house plant.

Kenilworth Ivy

This plant is a creeper with kidney-shaped, irregularly lobed leaves with shallow scallops on their edges. The miniature lilac-blue-snapdragon-type flowers have yellow throats. It's a native of the Alps and grows wild in the Appalachian mountains. Kenilworth Ivy is great for hanging baskets. New plants are easily grown because it is a creeper and roots wherever it touches moist ground.

Kangaroo Ivy

This "ivy" is an elegant trailing vine with large, shiny, saw-toothed leaves often six inches in length and shaped like an elm leaf. It does not grow too rapidly and needs cool temperatures.

Boston or Japanese Ivy

Many homes that seem to be covered with ivy in summer are really covered with Boston Ivy. This "ivy" is not a member of the *Hedera* family. It is a deciduous vine and makes a perfectly magnificent wall cover. Boston Ivy is vigorous and quick growing with large shiny grass-green leaves from two to seven inches wide. The leaves turn red and orange in autumn and can look spectacular against a wall.

Poison Ivy

I resent that this villainous plant has been given the name "Ivy". It is a shrub that crawls and climbs by means of aerial rootlets. The leaves consist of three somewhat oval, pointed leaflets, glossy on top and slightly hairy beneath. It has small greenish flowers that are followed by small, grayish round fruits, which remain on the plant all winter. In the fall the foliage turns red and orange. It should always be observed at as great a distance as possible. The extreme itching, burning, and blistering of the skin caused by the plant's toxicity can not only be painful but sometimes fatal.

Staging an Ivy Show

CHAPTER SIXTEEN

Planning and staging any flower show is great fun, but a lot of hard work; and an ivy show has its own particular problems. To make it easier for you I am reprinting in full the show schedule prepared by the Eastern Chapter of The American Ivy Society which was held at Longwood Gardens in Kennett Square, Pennsylvania on October 1, 1994. From it you can get not only ideas for your own show, but you will have the listing of the General Rules and Instructions, the requirements for the horticulture division, and the artistic design division. You will also have the scale of points for both container and cut specimens of ivy. Also included are entry forms for artistic and horticultural classes. And because The American Ivy Society is always looking for new enthusiastic members, included is a Society membership form.

With this as your guide you should have no trouble putting together your own ivy show.

THE AMERICAN IVY SOCIETY

1994 IVY SHOW

co-sponsored by:

**The American
Ivy Society**
Eastern Regional Chapter

and

**Longwood
Gardens, Inc.**

Saturday, October 1, 1994
11:00 am - 5:00 pm

LONGWOOD GARDENS
KENNETT SQUARE, PENNSYLVANIA

IVY SHOW COMMITTEE

Show Chairman............................Edward Broadbent

Registrar..Phyllis Dunham
(302) 378-2829

Classification & Placement..........Charles Dunham
Russell Windel

Horticulture Judges.......................Edward Broadbent
Charles Dunham
Phyllis Dunham
Elise Everhardt
Russell Windel

Artistic Schedule..........................Joy Ericson,
President, Delaware
Judges Council

Artistic Judges ....Gwendoly Hoch

Education Section ....Julie Padrutt
Russell Windell

Staging ....Edward Broadbent

Information...................................Elise Everhadt
(410) 747-6132
Russell Windell
(610) 363-6481

The American Ivy Society gratefully acknowledges the generous support of the Management and Staff of Longwood Gardens. The Society also extends its thanks to the patrons for their contributions.

The Easter Regional Chapter of the American Ivy Society meets four times per year. For more information contact Russell Windell (610) 363-6481.

GENERAL RULES AND INSTRUCTIONS

1. Entries will be staged on the fern floor of the Exhibition Hall in the Main Conservatory.
2. Entries should be brought to the Music Room (beige awning, rear of the Conservatories) between 7:00 am and 9:00 am.
3. The Exhibition Hall will be closed for judging from 9:15 to 10:30 am.
4. While Longwood Gardens and the American Ivy Society will exercise caution in safe guarding exhibits, they cannot assume any responsibility for damages to an entry.
5. Ribbons may be given:
   a) 1st-Blue Ribbon in all classes
   b) 2nd-Red Ribbon in all classes
   c) 3rd-Yellow Ribbon in all classes

   Special Awards that may be given:
   a) Longwood Award of Horticulture
   b) Suzanne Pierot Award of Topiary Excellence
   c) Bonsai Award of Merit
   d) American Ivy Society Artistic Award
   e) Tea Caddy Award from the British Ivy Society
   (awarded to Eastern Chapter Members only)
6. The Schedule is the law of the show.
7. The Horticulture section is judged by American Ivy Society accredited judges and the decision of the judges is final.
8. Exhibitors need not be American Ivy Society members.
9. Exhibitors must have grown plants entered in the Horticulture Division for a minimum of three months.
10. Ivies entered should be named cultivars.
11. Entries must be correctly named, entry tags filled out completely, and passed by the Classification Committee, before being placed on our show tables.
12. Exhibitors may make as many entries as desired in a class, provided each is a different cultivar.
13. No foreign substances may be used. (i.e. leaf polish, etc.)
14. Entries must be removed between 5:00 and 5:30 pm.

HORTICULTURE DIVISION

1. All entries must be correctly labeled and placed in the proper class.
2. All entries must have been grown by the exhibitor for a minimum of three months.
3. Classes may be subdivided at the discretion of the show committee.
4. All entries must be staged in a cly pot, unless otherwise stated.

A. OUTDOOR IVY CUT SPECIMENS
(3 specimens per entry, length not to exceed 18")
Class (1)-**Bird Foot**
Class (2)-**Curly**
Class (3)-**Heart-Shaped**
Class (4)-**Fan**
Class (5)-**Ivy-Ivy**
Class (6)-**Miniature**
Class (7)-**Oddity**
Class (8)-**Arborescent**
Class (9)-**Species other than (Hedera helix)**
Class (10)-**Non-Registered Ivy**
Class (11)-**Tea Caddy Challenge** - *This class is open to Eastern Chapter members only. Each exhibitor may enter only one entry of an outdoor cut specimen, from classes one through ten. The winner of the challenge will be presented with a Fortnum & Mason tea caddy full of English Tea. This award was presented to us by the British Ivy Society, with the condition that the award be held for one year, and that at the end of the year it must be returned full of English Tea for the next winner.*

B. POTTED IVY
Class (12)-**Bird Foot**
    (a) pots 4 1/2" or less
    (b) pots over 4 1/2"
Class (13)-**Curly**
    (a) pots 4 1/2" or less
    (b) pots over 4 1/2"
Class (14)-**Heart-Shaped**
    (a) pots 4 1/2" or less
    (b) pots over 4 1/2"

Class (15)-**Fan**
      (a) pots 4 1/2" or less
      (b) pots over 4 1/2"
Class (16)-**Ivy-Ivy**
      (a) pots 4 1/2" or less
      (b) pots over 4 1/2"
Class (17)-**Miniature**
      (a) pots 4 1/2" or less
      (b) pots over 4 1/2"
Class (18)-**Oddity**
      (a) pots 4 1/2" or less
      (b) pots over 4 1/2"
Class (19)-**Arborescent**
Class (20)-**Species other than** (*Hedera helix*)
Class (21)-**Non-Registered Ivy**

C. Hanging Basket
  Class (22)-**Green Ivy**
  Class (23)-**Variegated Ivy**

D. Ivy Topiary
  Class (24)-**Trained on Open-Frame**
  Class (25)-**Trained on Stuffed or Solid Frame**
      (*Plant rooted in the Pot*)
  Class (26)-**Grown on Stuffed or Solid Frame** (*No Container*)
  Class (27)-**Standard** (*Woody Stem*)

E. Bonsai (*must be in bonsai pot*)
  Class (28)-**Formal Upright** (*Broom, Umbrella, Flat-top*)
  Class (29)-**Informal Upright** (*Windswept, Slanting, Literati*)
  Class (30)-**Cascade or Semi-Cascade**
  Class (31)-**Free Style** (*Exposed root, Octopus, Multiple trunk*)

F. Other Artistic Forms
  Ivies may be grown in non-traditional container.

G. Education Section
  Entries by invitation only.

ARTISTIC DESIGN DIVISION

1. Ivy should be featured in all arrangements, unless otherwise stated, materials used may be designers choice.
2. Plant material for arrangements need not be grown by exhibitor.
3. Backgrounds, mats, sands, and accessories may be used unless otherwise stated.
4. The words arrangement, design, composition are considered synonymous.
5. No artificial flowers, fruits, foliage or candles permitted unless otherwise stated.
6. Stuffed birds, bird nests, or the flag of the United States may not be used.
7. Dried material may be painted or treated unless otherwise stated.
8. Plant material used may be listed on a 3x5 card, ivies to be named if possible. A short explanation of an interpretative design may be included.
9. No State Conservation Plant material may be used in arrangements.
10. Exhibitors must provide a substitute if unable to exhibit.
11. Four entries per class.

AN IVY ODYSSEY

*Class (1)-*The Year 2010

A creative design using predominately ivy and a few flowers permitted; fresh and/or dried material permitted. Dried material may be treated. Staged on a free standing pedestal 48" high with a base 12"x 12". No background permitted.

*Class (2)-*The Martians Are Coming

A design in a non-traditional container, featuring ivy incorporating fresh and/or dried plant material. Dried material may be treated. Few flowers permitted. To be staged on a table holding a beige colored Z shaped pedestal 8"x 8". No background permitted. Pedestal provided.

*Class (3)-*Voyage Into Fall

A composition featuring ivy using all fresh plant material, a few flowers permitted. To be staged on a table in a bamboo slatted niche 24"H x 20"W x 18"D. Background permitted.

*Class (4)-*A Space Odyssey

An arrangement featuring ivy and a few flowers, with fresh and/or dried plant material. To be staged on a table in a bamboo slatted niche 12"H x 10"W x 7"D. Background permitted.

SCALE OF POINTS

JUDGING IVY GROWN IN CONTAINERS

Scale of points from the American Ivy Society

A. FOLIAGE (35 POINTS)

1. **Leaf Pattern**
   a. Shape of leaves: Typical of cultivar and uniform over whole plant. i.e. Bird's Foot, Fan, Heart, etc.
   b. Size of leaves: Normal for variety and uniform over various growth cycles.
   c. Leaf Spacing: Even spacing and not missing segments, well distributed. Judging each cultivar according to its habit. i.e. self-branching vs. non self-branching.

2. **Texture of leaves**: Showing good culture, thickness according to cultivar. Venation may influence appearance of texture.

3. **Leaf Color:** Vibrant, healthy and typical of cultivar. Season of year and light intensity greatly influence color. Variegated and mixed variegated (mottled) are more difficult to obtain good color in all seasons. Browning and fading on old leaves is a color fault.

B. SYMMETRICAL BALANCE (30 POINTS)
Pots, baskets and hanging baskets should have good symmetrical growth patterns in all directions. Does not mean all must be the same length. Symmetry is easier to achieve with self-branching cultivars.

C. MATURITY OF PLANT (20 POINTS)
Plant should be full with sufficient size to show growth characteristics of cultivar. Hanging baskets should have some hanging shoots.

D. Condition and Grooming (15 Points)
Well-groomed, old leaves removed, pot clean, correct pot size, no evidence of insect or disease, spray residue or recent pruning.

Judging Cut Specimens of Ivy

A. **LEAF COLOR:** *Typical color for cultivar*   30

B. **CONDITION AND GROOMING:** *Clean, free of damage*   20

C. **LEAF PATTERN** *Typical of cultivar and growth habit*   20

D. **LEAF TEXTURE AND VEINING:** *Shiny, dull, rough
    or smooth according to cultivar*   15

E. **LEAF SPACING:** *Typical of cultivar and growth habits*   10

F. **NAME:** *Correct and legible label*   05
                                                        ———
    TOTAL POINTS   100

1994 ARTISTIC CLASSES ENTRY FORM

Exhibitor's Name (Please Print)   Last   First

Address

City   State   Zip   Phone

CLASS NUMBER   **TITLE**

1994 HORTICULTURAL CLASSES ENTRY FORM

CLASS NUMBER   **BOTANICAL & COMMON NAME**

Mail to *Phyllis Dunhan*
         AIS Ivy Show Registrar
         207 High Street, P.O. Box 176
         Odessa, DE 19730-176

1994 ARTISTIC CLASSES ENTRY FORM

Exhibitor's Name (Please Print) Last   First

_____

Address

_____

City   State   Zip   Phone

CLASS NUMBER   **BOTANICAL & COMMON NAME**

_____

_____

_____

_____

_____

_____

_____

_____

_____

_____

_____

_____

Mail to *Phyllis Dunhan*
         AIS Ivy Show Registrar
         207 High Street, P.O. Box 176
         Odessa, DE 19730-176

THE AMERICAN IVY SOCIETY
1994 MEMBERSHIP APPLICATION FORM

Please enter my membership for the 1994 calendar year.
As a member, during the calendar year I will receive:

- Three ivy newsletters, **Between the Vines**
- One **Ivy Journal**
- One ivy plant mailed in spring 1995. (*AIS is unable to ship the ivies to Canada or Mexico. Institutional and commercial may receive the ivy upon request.*)

MEMBERSHIP CATEGORIES
Please Circle Your Choice

CATEGORY	USA	CANADA & MEXICO Surface Mail	WESTERN HEMISPHERE Air
General membership, 1 year	$15.00	$20.00	$23.00
General membership, 3 years	$40.00	$55.00	$64.00
Family membership, 1 year	$20.00	$25.00	$28.00
Commercial membership, 1 year	$50.00	$60.00	$65.00
Institutional membership, 1 year	$25.00	$30.00	$33.00

Lifetime Membership, $250.00
For Chapter Membership information, please contact AIS, address at bottom.

Membership rated quoted are in United States dollars. Make payment in check, international draft or an American Express money order, payable to:
The American Ivy Society, Inc.
Mail to: **Daphne Pfaff, Membership Chairman,**
696 Sixteenth Ave. South Naples, FL 33940, U.S.A.

❏ **New Membership**   ❏ **Renewal**   Amount Enclosed_____

_____
Name of Organization (if applicable)

_____
Contact Person's Name

_____
Address

_____
City   State   Zip

_____
Country

In order for members to have contact with one another within their own region or while traveling, we will be printing a membership list with address in *Between the Vines* once a year. If you wish not to have your address printed please check here. ❏

Sources

Ivies

Gilson Gardens
Mark Gibson
3059 US Route 20
Perry, OH 44081
Wholesale & Retail
Mail Order
216/ 259-4845
FAX 216/ 259-2378

Ivies of the World
Time and Judy Rankin
P.O. Box 408
Weirsdale, FL 32195
Wholesale & Retail
Walk-in by Appointment
Mail Order
904/ 821-2201 (Days)
904/ 821-2322 (Eves)

Pheasant Hill Nursery
David Reed
665 Route 524
Allentown, NJ 08501
Retail
Walk-In
609/ 259-3441

Hedera, Etc.
Russell Windle
P.O. Box 461
Lionville, PA 19393
Wholesale & Retail
Mail Order
Custom Ivy Propagation
610/ 970-9175

Merry Gardens
Mary Ellen Ross
P.O. Box 595
Camden, ME 04843
Wholesale & Retail
Mail Order
Walk In
Ivies & Topiaries
207/ 236-2121

Riverbend Nursery
Jim Snyder
Route 1, Box 628
Riner, VA 24149
Wholesale & Retail
Mail Order
Ivies & Topiary
703/ 763-3362

Samia Rose Topiary
Patricia Riley Hammer
P.O. Box 23-12081
Encinitas, CA 92023
Consulting
Properties Custom Design
Finished Topiary
Custom Ivy Propagation
619/ 434-0460

Schickenberg Nursery
Kristine Manfred
54 Princeton Ave.
Half Mood, Bay, CA 94019
Commercial Wholesale
Finished Topiary & Frames
Consulting, Custom Design
415/ 728-3817

Wholesale Only

Anmar Greenhouses
Tony Alkemade
RR #5, Welland Road
Fenwick, Ontario,
Canada L0SIC0
Ivies and topiary
(905) 892-6916

Arbors of Ivy
Rose McMillan
2150 W. Lime Street
DeLand, FL 32720
Cut ivy for floral use
(904) 734-2849

Batson's Greenhouse, Inc.
Tom Landers
PO Box 641
Zellwood, FL 32798-0641
Ivies and finished topiary
(407) 886-4948
Fax (407) 886-4948

The Berkshire Ivy gardens
Michael Shanley
835 Simonds Road
Williamstown, MA 01267

Evergreen Nursery
1220 Dowdy Road
Athens, GA 30606
(706) 548-7781

Foremost Foliage/
MAYACROPS
Randy Natalino
8457 N.W. 66th Street
Miami, FL 33166
1-(800) 421-8986
Fax (305) 591-4093

Hopkins Nursery, Inc.
Frances Hopkins
5326 72nd Ave., S.E.
Salem, OR 97301
(503) 581-8915

The Ivy Farm, Inc.
Richard Davis
PO Box 114
Locustville, VA 23404
(804) 787-4096

Iverson Perennials
Ron Iverson
Rt. 1 Box 326 B
Orange, VA 22960
(703) 672-9088

Live Oak Greenhouses
Hans & Maria Schoenfliess
1343 South Live Oak Park Rd.
Falbrook, CA 92028
Ivy and Topiary
(619) 728-0645

Twixwood Nursery
Dennis Wentworth
4669 E. Hillcrest Drive
Berrien Spring, MI 49107
(616) 471-7408

Vine Acres Nursery, Inc.
Wendell Davis
PO Box 317
Clarcona, FL 32710
Ivies and Topiaries
Frames, Custom Design
(407) 886-5900

Topiaries/Supplies

Cliff Finch's Zoo
Cliff Finch
P.O. Box 54
16923 N. Friant Rd.
Wholesale & Retail
Topiary Supplies
Custom Design
207/ 236-2121

Merry Gardens
Mary Ellen Ross
P.O. Box 595
Camden, ME 04843
Wholesale & Retail

Metal Creations
Milt Neely
777 W. 12th Street
Ogden, UT 84404
Wholesale & Retail
Frames
801/ 621-0112

Topiaries Unlimited
Joyce Held
R.E. 2, Box 40C
Pownal, VT 05261
Frames, Topiaries
802/ 823-5536

Samia Rose Topiary
Patricia Riley Hammer
P.O. Box 23-1208
Encinitas, CA 92023
Consulting, Commercial
Properties, Custom Design
Finished Topiary
Custom Ivy Propagation
619/ 434-0460

Topiary, Inc.
Carole Buyton & Mia Hardcastle
41 Bering Street
Tampa, FL 33606
Wholesale & Retail
Frames, Topiaries
Custom Design
813/ 254-3229

For more information contact:
The American Ivy Society
Ohio 513/ 862-4700   Florida 813/ 261-0785

Ivy Regional and Display Collections

California
Mendocino Coast Botanical Gardens
Western Regional Standard Reference Collection
18820 N. Highway 1, Ft. Bragg, CA 95437
Tel: 707 964-4352

Florida
Sugar Mill Botanic Garden
950 Old Sugar Mill Rd. (West of US 1)
Ft. Orange, FL
Tel: 904 788-3645

Maryland
Brookside Garden
Display Collection
1500 Glenallan Ave.
Wheaton, MD 20902
Tel: 301 929-6509

Illinois
Chicago Botanic Garden
Hardiness Trials
P.O. Box 400 Lake-Cook Rd. (East of Edens Expressway)
Glencoe, IL 60022
Tel: 708 835-8251

Ohio
American Ivy Society Hardiness Trials
Gillia and Don Hawke
205 Summit St.
Lebanon, Ohio 45036
Tel: 513 932-3318

Tennessee
University of Tennessee
Dept. of Ornamental Horticulture,
Display Collection and Hardiness Trials
P.O. Box 1071, Knoxville, TN 37901
Tel: 615 974-7324

Virginia
Lewis Ginter Botanic Garden
Display Collection
1800 Lakeside Avenue
Richmond, VA 23228
Tel: 804 262-9887

River Farm
Headquarters of American Horticultural Society
Display Collection
7931 East Boulevard Drive
Alexandria, VA 22308
Tel: 703 768-5700

Please telephone before visiting.

$\mathcal{I}ndex$

Notes